Woman to Woman

Woman to Woman

Selected Talks from the BYU Women's Conferences

Camilla Eyring Kimball

Norma B. Ashton • Barbara B. Smith

Grethe Ballif Peterson • Maren M. Mouritsen

Patricia T. Holland • Elaine A. Cannon

Libby R. Hirsh • Ida Smith

Karen Lynn Davidson • Ardeth Greene Kapp

Tamara M. Quick • Beverly Campbell

Sally H. Barlow • Marilyn Arnold

Belle S. Spafford

Deseret Book Company
Salt Lake City, Utah

©1986 Deseret Book Company
All rights reserved
Printed in the United States of America

No part of this book may be reproduced in any
form or by any means without permission in writing
from the publisher, Deseret Book Company,
P.O. Box 30178, Salt Lake City, Utah 84130.
Deseret Book is a registered trademark of
Deseret Book Company, Inc.

First printing March 1986
Second printing July 1986

Library of Congress Cataloging-in-Publication Data
Main entry under title:

Woman to woman

    Includes index.
    1. Women—Religious life—Addresses, essays,
lectures.   2. Women—Conduct of life—Addresses,
essays, lectures. I. Kimball, Camilla E. II. Brigham
Young University.
BV4527.W59   1986   248.4'89332043   86-2048
ISBN 0-87579-035-6

Contents

Keys for a Woman's Progression
CAMILLA EYRING KIMBALL 1

For Such a Time as This, the Time Is Now
NORMA B. ASHTON 13

Blueprints for Living
BARBARA B. SMITH 27

A Woman's Role and Destiny
IDA SMITH 43

Drifting, Dreaming, Directing
ARDETH GREENE KAPP 49

Daughters of God
ELAINE A. CANNON 65

Priesthood and Sisterhood:
An Equal Partnership
GRETHE BALLIF PETERSON 75

Dare to Make a Difference
BEVERLY CAMPBELL 85

The Savior: An Example for Everyone
KAREN LYNN DAVIDSON 101

Within Whispering Distance of Heaven
PATRICIA T. HOLLAND 115

Contents

Responsible Assertiveness: How to Get
Along without Getting Up or Getting Out
SALLY H. BARLOW, TAMARA M. QUICK 125

Scholars of the Scriptures
MAREN M. MOURITSEN 135

Being Well Balanced: A Key
to Mental Health
LIBBY R. HIRSH, M.D. 149

Reading and Loving Literature
MARILYN ARNOLD 181

Appendix:
The American Woman's Movement
BELLE S. SPAFFORD 199

Index 213

Preface

Each year since 1975, Brigham Young University has sponsored a woman's conference, which annually attracts thousands of women to the BYU campus to hear outstanding presentations on subjects of concern to Latter-day Saint women. The speakers include both men and women, individuals who have achieved in community and church service, family life, and their professions.

From these conferences, Deseret Book has selected fourteen addresses for *Woman to Woman*. Included as an appendix is a talk on the American women's movement, delivered at a meeting in New York City by Belle S. Spafford, former president of the National Council of Women and for many years general president of the Relief Society in The Church of Jesus Christ of Latter-day Saints.

These talks originally appeared in four paperbound volumes published by Brigham Young University: *Blueprints for Living* (two volumes), *Ye Are Free to Choose,* and *For Such a Time as This.* Editor of these volumes was Dr. Maren M. Mouritsen, former dean of student life at BYU and an adviser to the ASBYU women's office, and most recently an assistant vice-president of the university.

The first volume of *Blueprints for Living* had a foreword by President Spencer W. Kimball. His words summarize well both the purposes of the women's conferences and the intent of *Woman to Woman:* "The very number and nature of the challenges in today's world give rise to the need to assure ourselves in The Church of Jesus Christ of Latter-day Saints that we are doing all we can to prepare our wonderful women to meet those challenges that they, and all of us, face. . . .

"Believing as we do in the special place of women, both in this life and in eternity, the Church welcomes every appropriate effort to help women reach their great possibilities. Our Father in Heaven has a perfect love which he bestows upon each of his spirit daughters and sons, for God is clearly no respecter of persons.

"It is a great blessing to be a woman in the Church today, but with that blessing comes great responsibility. Meeting that responsibility will require service, study, prayer, and a humble seeking of the Spirit of the Lord to guide in the quest for wisdom and knowledge. . . . May God bless you, the sisters of the Church, as you continue your life's journey."

Keys for a
Woman's Progression

CAMILLA EYRING KIMBALL

first came to Provo in 1912, a frightened, bewildered refugee. My family had lived in Colonia Juárez, Mexico, and was forced to leave when revolutionaries in the Mexican Civil War threatened the Mormon colonies in Chihuahua and Sonora. I was seventeen when we fled by train to El Paso, leaving practically everything behind. I recall how one of the revolutionaries brazenly lifted a woman's purse from her arm with the barrel of his rifle as she boarded the train. It was a traumatic experience for all of us to leave our homes and start again in a new country. For a few days we were housed in stalls in a lumberyard in El Paso, Texas. The curious came to stare at us. Finally Father came out of Mexico on horseback, and we rented some rooms. My uncle, Carl Eyring, was in Provo attending BYU along with his sister. They wrote, inviting me to come live with them and to finish high school at BYU. This was most generous of them, for they were hard-pressed for funds enough to keep the two of them in school.

The next two years at BYU left me with indelible memories. They were hard, poverty-ridden years, but a time of great personal growth. I learned and prepared myself for employment as a teacher of home economics in the Church academies. I came to love BYU, and through the years I have watched with a thrill as this school has grown tremendously and grown in size and in worldwide influence.

I read the school papers and envy you the many wonderful cultural and intellectual opportunities. I have thought that when my husband and I get to retirement age, perhaps we can come to Provo and be active participants in the wonderful programs available here. I hope each of you has some sense of what a great privilege it is to be part of this institution and that you make every day count in learning and in making lasting friendships. I appreciate this invitation to be with you at the beginning of this conference and share some ideas of how women can best fulfill their calling in life.

The Lord expects men and women alike, first of all, to grow in spirituality—that is, to worship him; to gain understanding of the kind of being he is and wants us to become; to develop deep, abiding faith; and to live by divine principles of conduct. No other school in the whole world is so richly endowed with the resources to teach the whole truth—to teach the important, eternal verities as well as the worldly knowledge we need for vocation and for enjoyment of life. Of all we learn in life, the single most important knowledge we can attain is a firm testimony of the Lord Jesus Christ as our Savior and an understanding of the path he would have us follow.

Sometimes we are accused of being boastful in declaring that we belong to the only true church. But we say it not in pride but in gratitude, considering ourselves blessed to have been born members of the Church or to have had a favorable opportunity to hear the gospel preached so that we would understand and accept it. We reject no truth or good to be found anywhere, but we are anxious to share that added truth which we have. All truth is a part of the gospel. Truth is things as they were, as they are, and as they will be. We are not so arrogant as to assert that the Church program is perfect, for it continues to add programs to meet the changing times, nor would we say that its members are perfect. We have a long way to go before we have become all that the Lord wants us to be. But we do say to all who will listen, "Here is more truth than can be found anywhere else in this world because God has established his church to teach his children as much as is within their capacity to learn," and we say to others, "Come and share with us!"

Many years ago, when we were vacationing in Long Beach, California, I went to the public library to look for books to read. As I browsed through the shelves, a strange woman came up beside me and, with no preliminary introduction, said to me in a demanding voice, "Are you saved?" Taken aback, I paused a second to consider. Then I answered, "Well, I'm working on it." With firm conviction, she admonished, "You'd better accept Christ now and be saved, or you may be too late!" I have thought about this encounter many times since, and my answer to the question would of necessity still be the same today: "I'm working on it." Of course, our salvation depends upon our acceptance of Christ, but also on our continual progress and our remaining faithful to the end. Salvation is a process, not an event.

A major part of that process is in service. King Benjamin said, "When ye are in the service of your fellow beings ye are only in the service of your God." (Mosiah 2:17.) What shall we serve? Our first obligation is to our families.

So far as we know, the Church organization may not be found in heaven, but families will be. God joined Adam and Eve in the holy bonds of marriage even before they were mortal and commanded them to cleave to one another. God has through all ages fostered the family, giving to men the sealing power so that families can be joined for eternity. The importance of our finding worthy companions and of temple marriage cannot be overestimated when we realize that our eternal destiny depends in part upon this sacred ordinance. Without it, we cannot have fulness of joy. With it, the future is boundless. There are some who, through no fault of their own, do not have that opportunity in this life, but no one worthy of these blessings will be denied them indefinitely. Life stretches beyond mortality, and those who live worthily will find fulfillment in the hereafter.

As husbands and wives, parents and children, our foremost duty and opportunity for service is to one another. President McKay said that "no other success can compensate for failure in

3

the home." We must take advantage of every effective means to strengthen home ties.

The family home evening program has long been a part of the Church plan. I remember well as a child the occasions in our family when we gathered together and each child, beginning with the youngest, had a part on the home evening program. These are happy memories. When my brothers and sisters get together even now, we often reminisce about those times, repeating with laughter the poems and songs we performed back in those days.

It was fun to hear my brother Henry sing in monotone,

> What can little bodies do?
> Like us little lispers,
> Full of life and mischief, too,
> And prone to noisy whispers.

And Joe's oft-repeated contribution as a little three-year-old was,

> Three little rabbits went out to run,
> Up hill and down hill
> Oh, what fun!

The songs the family sang together are still our favorites. Some of them were folk songs brought from England by our great-grandmother. We still sing these with our grandchildren, and these are traditions that bind the family together.

In recent years more definite and concerted effort is being made to perfect the program. We have come to realize that Monday family home evening should be as regular and important a part of our life as attendance at sacrament meeting, that it is worth sacrifices to keep this time special for those close to us.

Many people outside the Church are recognizing and adopting the family home evening program as a tool to strengthen their families. Some time ago my husband spoke at a convention of young business executives and their wives at Sun Valley, Idaho. None of them were members of the Church, but several of them came personally to express appreciation for our family home evening manual, which they were using with their families. A first major effort by the Church to reach the world with this message, the nationwide television program on home evening, had much greater response than anticipated. Thousands of requests for the home evening booklet were received from all parts of the country. What a chance, by precept and example, to have important impact on the lives of our neighbors!

We are by no means the only ones to recognize the importance of the family. Dr. Earl Schaefer at the University of North Carolina has affirmed that "parents and the home environment are more critical to a child's educational success than schools and teachers are." Three years of research has produced "a tremendous amount of evidence that parents' involvement with the child has the greatest impact in achievement, in curiosity, persistence—even creativity." It has long been said that children whose parents read aloud to them learn to read better and with greater enjoyment than children who do not have such experience. Also, that those coming from homes where books are read, ideas discussed, and art appreciated prove to be better students than those who have missed these experiences.

I am sure most of us could bear testimony to the value of our home environment, where family ideals were inculcated in us that provide lasting guidelines for our lives.

Young people anticipating marriage and family should keep these findings firmly in mind. Mothers with small children cannot overestimate the importance of the mother's place in the home with her children. Whoever shares that time with the children will largely determine their character and shape their lives. What a challenge for women!

I still have a vivid memory of my mother sitting at the table after supper in the evening with the lighted coal-oil lamp and an open book before her. As she read aloud to us, she at the same time was knitting stockings for the family. The click of the knitting needles punctuated the stories she read. From her example, I learned to love books and to reject idleness.

Good books were always an important part of our home life. I remember, though, one day when I was small, I came home from the library with the book *Camille* by Emile Zola, anticipating reading it because the title of the book was so much like my name. The minute Mama saw the book, she exclaimed, "Oh, no, dear, you don't want to read that book." She promptly returned it to the library. A good many years later I read it and then realized that she was quite right in thinking I was much too young for it the first time. I am grateful that she loved me enough to establish standards in our home. The existence of reasonable rules is almost as important as their content.

Rita Chapman of Dallas, Texas, is quoted in the *Church News* as follows:

> I am totally convinced that once a woman has borne a child, she owes that child herself more than anything else in the first five years of his life. . . .
>
> I fear that raising emotion-starved and love-starved children can produce calloused, robotized adults—people who follow the group in straight lines and do exactly what everyone else is doing, because someone has said it is time.
>
> I fear for the working mother who is deluded to believe that some kind, patient woman will tend to her child's emotional needs until she can take over, that someone else will see that her child discovers he is unique, until she can pick him up at the end of the day—when she is perhaps so tired that the best he can hope to hear is, "It's time to go to bed."
>
> I fear for the future of the child whose hunger for love and recognition must be satisfied in large groups. I beg mothers to wake up, to experience the precious dawning of their child's life with him. Evening comes quickly—but in the evening may be too late. (*Church News,* August 14, 1976.)

The impact of what parents do in the home extends beyond the home, to community and nation. Michael Novak, in *Harper's* magazine, said:

> Throughout history, nations have been able to survive a multiplicity of disasters—invasions, famines, earthquakes, epidemics, depressions, but they have never been

able to survive the disintegration of the family. The family is the seed bed of economic skills, money habits, attitude toward work, and the art of financial independence. It is a stronger agency of education than the school and stronger for religious training than the church. What strengthens the family strengthens the society; . . . if things go well with the family, life is worth living. When the family falters, life falls apart. (Michael Novak, "Family Out of Favor," *Harper's* 252 [April 1976]: 37-40.)

We are in a period when the great propaganda machines are telling us that for a woman to choose a career in home and family is somehow demeaning, and that self-respect demands that she pursue a profession of law or medicine or business. But rather than directing both marriage partners away from the home, we need to encourage both to make the strengthening of the family their primary concern. There is challenge, accomplishment, and satisfaction enough for anyone in this greatest educational endeavor—the home.

In the rural society of my childhood, we often lived close enough to grandparents, uncles and aunts, brothers and sisters, and cousins to use their physical and psychic resources to supplement our own. When we needed help, they were there. But in our highly mobile society today, this extended family is rarely so available. And today fellow Church members often fill that function. The visiting teacher and home teacher programs can provide support of this kind. Every family in the Church has two pairs of teachers who, taken together, should visit that home at least two dozen times a year with a spiritual message and a constant reminder that others care for us. We are responsible for one another. I help you and you help me. These visiting programs offer some of the strongest evidence that we truly are willing to serve one another and that the Church is an extension of the family idea.

In the Church organization, there are ample opportunities for both men and women. I have felt no deprivation in not holding the priesthood. I feel only gratitude that I can, with my husband and sons, receive all of its blessings without my having to assume many of its responsibilities. I have had teaching and leadership positions enough to give me full range for my abilities. In my fifty years as a visiting teacher of the Relief Society, I have had some of my richest human and spiritual experiences. In times of sickness and sorrow, there are very specific needs. In other homes you may be the only contact an inactive family has with the Church. The hand of friendship and fellowship is often the means of reactivation of these families.

It is clear to me that from an eternal perspective, it does not matter where we serve but only how faithfully we serve. To each of us who has a calling as a teacher of families in the Church, I say be faithful and supportive, fulfilling that responsibility to the best of your abilities. And to each of us who is in a family being taught, I say let us make our teachers welcome and allow them to serve us, for in so doing we both shall be blessed.

If we want to give effective service to our families and our neighbors, as we are commanded to do, we must develop ourselves to our full potential. We need to enlarge our intellect and perfect our character. We need to become more Christlike.

The pursuit of knowledge, which is characteristic of a university, is not only permissible, it is part of the gospel plan for us. The revelation given through the Prophet Joseph Smith in section 88 of the Doctrine and Covenants sets the scope of our study:

> Teach ye diligently and my grace shall attend you, that you may be instructed more perfectly in theory, in principle, in doctrine, in the law of the gospel, in all things that pertain unto the kingdom of God, that are expedient for you to understand;
> Of things both in heaven and in the earth, and under the earth; things which have been, things which are, things which must shortly come to pass; things which are at home, things which are abroad; the wars and the perplexities of the nations, and the judgments which are on the land; and a knowledge also of countries and kingdoms—
> That ye may be prepared in all things when I shall send you again to magnify the calling whereupon I have called you, and the mission with which I have commissioned you. . . .

And as all have not faith, seek ye diligently and teach
one another words of wisdom; yea, seek ye out of the best
books words of wisdom; seek learning, even by study and
also by faith. (D&C 88:78-80, 118.)

My feeling is that each of us has the potential for special
accomplishment in some field. The opportunities for women to
excel are greater today than ever before. We should all be
resourceful and ambitious, expanding our interests. Forget
self-pity and look for mountains to climb. Everyone has problems. The challenge is to cope with those problems and get our
full measure of joy from life. These "words of wisdom" from
books are a means to that end.

Here and now you are much engrossed in textbooks, which
are often tedious but important to the task of preparing for a
specific career. They are keys that open doors, windows that
open on life.

Some of the delightful pleasures of life are in continuing
education in our mature years and in collecting and reading
fine books. Continue to pick up interesting information in history, current events, the arts. There are various areas that we
may miss in the few years we are enrolled in college, and learning confined to four years is soon out of date.

Through the years I have found it stimulating to be enrolled
in a college class or two each year. The stimulation of association with young people helps keep one alive. For some years in
Arizona I worked in the city library, which was sponsored by
the Federated Women's Club. I helped in the selection of books
and found this a challenge to keep up with current literature. I
still belong to one or another of the book clubs that bring a
variety of reading material into our home, and I do make a concerted effort to select worthwhile books.

And beyond books, learning means keeping the mind open
to all kinds of experience. Travel when you have a chance.
Travel with an open mind, an alert eye, and a wish to understand other people, other places. That fits us all the better for
most of life's callings.

When our children were young, every summer we, with

them, made a trip by car to visit the different areas of America, east, west, north, and south. This way we gained a greater appreciation for our great country. Going to Rotary International conventions, especially to Mexico and Europe, broadened our outlook. We worked at touring, seeing countries and people in detail. It has been my privilege, with my husband, to visit the members of the Church in countries all around the world. This has been an opportunity to get close to the people, to feel their needs.

The first fundamental need of every person is the indispensability of love, the feeling of being of value to others. Our interdependence with others is the most encompassing fact of human reality. We need each other.

Much unhappiness has been suffered by those people who have never recognized that it is as necessary to make themselves into whole and harmonious personalities as to keep themselves clean, healthy, and financially solvent. Wholeness of the mind and spirit is not a quality conferred by nature or by God. It is like health and knowledge. Man has the capacity to attain it, but to achieve it depends on our own efforts. It needs a long, deliberate effort of the mind and the emotions and even the body. During our earthly life the body gradually slows down, but the mind has the capacity to grow even more lively and active. The chief limitations confronting us are not age or sex or race or money. They are laziness, shortsightedness, and lack of self-esteem. Those who avoid learning or abandon it find that life becomes dry, but when the mind is alert, life is luxuriant. No learner has ever run short of subjects to explore. You can live most rewardingly by attaining and preserving the joy of learning and serving.

Let me say in summary that with all the other knowledge that enriches our lives, let us not forget to include the knowledge of the gospel of Jesus Christ. When we think how fervently earthly parents want their children to grow up in faithfulness, we can appreciate in some small measure the great desire our Heavenly Father has that his beloved children may find their way back to him. Living the gospel is not the easiest way of life, but it is the most rewarding way.

I am grateful for the understanding we have of our responsibility to become Godlike in character, to love our children and neighbors as he loves us. The family is important enough to call for our best efforts—no profession is more noble than homemaking. The fulness of respect from good men and from God comes to those who fit themselves to serve and then serve one another—and family first of all—with love.

Nephi wrote: "Wherefore, ye must press forward with a steadfastness in Christ, having a perfect brightness of hope, and a love of God and of all men. Wherefore, if ye shall press forward, feasting upon the word of Christ, and endure to the end, behold, thus saith the Father: Ye shall have eternal life." (2 Nephi 31:20.) This is the greatest gift God has to offer.

I am grateful for the example set by Christ and for his great atoning sacrifice. I know that he lives. My prayer for us all is that we may follow his admonition to seek divine perfection in our lives and endure faithfully and joyfully to the end of our lives so that we may worthily claim our reward in his kingdom.

Camilla Eyring Kimball grew up in northern Mexico and attended Brigham Young Academy in Provo, Utah. In 1917 she began teaching at Gila Academy in Arizona; it was there that she met and married Spencer W. Kimball, who would later become twelfth president of The Church of Jesus Christ of Latter-day Saints. This address was given at a BYU devotional assembly in February 1977.

For Such a Time as This, the Time Is Now

NORMA B. ASHTON

I have a favorite General Authority. In one of his talks he said, "Some spend so much time getting ready to live for an unknown future that they suddenly discover there is no time left to live." This has been a fairly common theme in recent times. And yet the pendulum has swung far to the other extreme in many segments of today's society: ignore inhibitions; do what you feel like doing; discard any moral values that are restrictive; live for the pleasure of the moment.

In considering these pleasures of the moment, it is well to remember that the "nows" determine to a great extent the "forevers." For this reason, even though we want and must enjoy the "right nows," we should keep tomorrow and forever in perspective. Waiting for a brighter future may cause us to lose a beautiful today.

Our children smile as they remember the little sayings I used to put over a lesson as they were growing up, but now I find them using them in their own homes occasionally. One such saying is, "That which is good, you pay for before you get it. That which is bad, you pay for after you take it, and the price is usually higher than you expect."

Let me illustrate with the story of Maggie Bellows, who was an internationally known journalist. Her articles appeared in many papers. Foreign countries invited her for seminars. Her husband was associate editor of the *New York Times*. In her home in Phoenix she entertained heads of state, movie stars, and many important authors and journalists. During one June Conference she came to Salt Lake City to write an article on the activities of Mormon youth. I was asked to be her hostess.

She was so important that the First Presidency gave her a private interview. Some of the women leaders of our auxiliaries held a luncheon for her. She did not smoke in the Church Office Building, but always as she walked out she lit a cigarette. (Now this is not a Word of Wisdom story.) After a long, full day I took her to the Hotel Utah for a lovely dinner. To me the food was so welcome, but as I ate she stirred hers around a little and smoked. Then she excused herself with these words: "I am going to call my seventy-year-old mother in Phoenix. She is dying of lung cancer, and if she is conscious I will go to her bedside; if not, I must go on to New York." On returning to the table, she reported that her mother was still in a coma and asked if I could take her to catch her flight to New York.

About five years later we were in Phoenix. I picked up a local paper, and the headline of one of the articles read "Maggie Bellows Memorial Fund." Startled, I read on and found that this great journalist had died of lung cancer at age fifty. A memorial was being established in her honor. Then I remembered very clearly a statement she had made that evening we had dinner together. "I smoke a lot, but it is about my only vice. Don't you think the Lord will forgive me if that's all I do?" I remember saying, "I suppose he will."

This woman had everything to live for. She was productive and successful; she had a good marriage and admiration from many; but with all her warnings, she let her desires for today wipe out many good tomorrows. I think the Lord will forgive her, but I also think she paid a much bigger price than she intended—twenty years less of the good life that could have been hers. Certainly to enjoy the "nows," we must consider and pay the price.

In John 10:10 Jesus says, "I am come that they might have

life, and that they might have it more abundantly." Our challenge is to learn to have the abundant life today *and* tomorrow. For our purposes today, let's think together about ways that an abundant life can be a daily experience, for inevitably, that lifestyle will spill over into the tomorrows.

The "if only" trap catches us all at times. "If only I had money or power or influence, or a slim, trim figure, or a beautiful face, or great talent, or a bigger home, or a more prestigious job, I would be happy." Yet on every hand we find people who have some or all of these things, and we are aware that there is no happiness in their daily lives.

Some time ago I read a statement made by one of the richest, most beautiful women of our time, Elizabeth Taylor. She said, "I have never known one really happy day in my life."

Avoiding the present moment is almost a disease in our culture. Many of us condition ourselves to sacrifice the present for the future. There was a girl on vacation in Hawaii who spent all her time at the pool or the beach turning and tanning, even though she was often uncomfortable. She missed the palms, the beautiful scenery, even other fun activities just so she could go back to her office and show off her tan. Many others say they will be happy when the mortgage is paid or when the children get into school, or go on missions, or find mates.

Can we analyze ourselves? Do we feel that we must sacrifice ourselves for the future? When that future does arrive, it becomes today, and we will probably go on using it to prepare for some other wonderful tomorrow. Tomorrow's happiness is so elusive. Life is what happens to you when you have other plans. Our task is to find the abundant life along the way, to pause and relish each twenty-four hours that we are given by our Father in heaven.

Eric Fromm writes, "Happiness is not a gift of the gods." If that is the case, what can we do to prevent our losing this beautiful today?

Three verbs come to mind that might be helpful as we plan our attack on achieving great todays: *loving, learning,* and *living.* These are rather vague words, so let's elaborate on them using more specific examples.

The eighth Psalm is a good starting place for loving. It gives us reason to love ourselves. "What is man, that thou art mindful of him? and the son of man, that thou visitest him? For thou hast made him a little lower than the angels, and hast crowned him with glory and honour." (Verses 4-5.) Wordsworth wrote, "Trailing clouds of glory do we come from God, who is our home." "A little lower than the angels." "Trailing clouds of glory." What do these truths tell you about yourself?

All of us come to earth as God's creation. Each has an innate nobility. Then worldly falsehoods disseminated by the father of lies start to clutter up our lives. "You aren't any good." "You are not worthy." "You must fit this mold." "You can't do anything right." "Try harder—think less; you can't improve." And on and on. Satan tries to jerk away those clouds of glory, and he is good at jerking.

To love ourselves, we must realize who we are and examine our feelings about ourselves. It is our obligation and opportunity to eliminate the negative and to nourish our real selves with humble pride and conduct worthy of one a little lower than the angels. Self-worth can't be verified by others. You are worthy because you say it is so. I realize this isn't an easy assignment. Even a prophet has to struggle for this realization.

Spencer W. Kimball and Harold B. Lee were close friends. They went into the Quorum of the Twelve just a few weeks apart. President Kimball said he always admired this friend so very much; in fact, he almost envied President Lee for his talents. He took every occasion to tell Elder Lee how he felt. Often he would say, "Harold, I wish I could play the organ as you do." "Harold, you speak so well. I wish I could do as well." "Harold, you can see the gist of a problem in such a short time. I wish my mind were so clear." Then, related President Kimball, in one of their weekly meetings in the temple President Lee made a fine presentation to the other members of the Twelve. As they walked out of the temple together, again President Kimball turned to his friend and said, "You did a magnificent job with your report this morning. I wish I could do as well as you do." "Well," said President Kimball with a twinkle in his eyes, "I guess Harold had had enough. He stopped, put his hands on his hips, and, looking me straight in the eye, said, 'Spencer, the Lord doesn't want you to be a Harold B. Lee. All he wants is for you to be the best Spencer W. Kimball you can be.'" With a smile on his face, President Kimball said, "Ever since then I have just tried to be the best Spencer W. Kimball I can be." And would you say that he has been very successful doing that? That is an answer for all of us. All the Lord asks of us is to be the best we can be with what we have.

Eliminating negative thoughts and actions about ourselves can be a difficult task. We think we have to tear ourselves down. Somehow we think a gracious "thank you" for a personal compliment is egotistical, so we deny the kind words. Have you ever told someone how nice she looked only to have her say, "Oh, I look terrible, I haven't had time to do my hair"? Or when you compliment her on her lovely dress, you hear these words: "Oh, this old thing. I bought it for almost nothing at the cut-rate store." Or if you say, "You gave a good talk," the reply is, "I was frightened to death. It was terrible."

Let me illustrate with an article titled "Don't Sell Yourself Short":

> At a party I was much attracted to a pretty girl with a charming personality. A fellow who was doing publicity for a big diamond firm sauntered up to her, spoke of her graceful posture, and told her she was so pretty. He said he would like to use her as a model for photographs to advertise some of his jewels. She could pose with a million dollars' worth of diamonds in necklaces and bracelets. She laughed and said she would love to. "But," she added, "my hands are awful." And she spread them out to him with her fingers wide apart.
>
> Up to that moment I hadn't noticed her hands, which were a bit red and rather large. But after that uncalled-for remark, I almost forgot about her hair, which was so lovely, her large violet eyes, and engaging smile. I saw nothing but her hands. She seemed to have so many hands. You don't have to ring bells and wave flags in an attempt to advertise your good points, but must you throw brickbats? (*Reader's Digest,* August 1954, p. 14.)

17

We don't have to degrade ourselves in public. We don't have to point out our flaws. We do need to work on them. If there is something you don't like and can change it, work on changing. If not, accept what God has given you and work with what you have. "For all have not every gift given unto them; for there are many gifts, and to every man is given a gift by the Spirit of God. To some is given one, and to some is given another, that all may be profited thereby." (D&C 46:11-12.)

As Spencer W. Kimball was taught, a copy is never as valuable as the original. Each of us is an original made by God, and we diminish ourselves and our Maker when we question our worth.

We mistakenly think that things or people make us unhappy. But really that is not so. We make ourselves unhappy by the way we let ourselves act or react to the words or deeds of others. As our love for ourselves grows, and we don't feel the need to justify and explain our actions, we can use our energy in also loving others.

My husband often says, "Never let yourself be offended by someone who is learning his job." Because we are a lay church and because we all change jobs at what seem to be brief intervals, we are all constantly learning how to fulfill new assignments. No one should ever let himself be hurt by a brother or sister in the gospel. We are each too worthy to be upset by someone else.

The second word we mentioned for happy todays is *learning*. Intellectuality itself probably can't get us to the celestial kingdom. It must be coupled with spirituality, virtue, and application. There is an old Persian proverb I like: "One pound of learning requires ten pounds of common sense to apply it."

In order to move ahead day by day, we need to be aware of the world around us. We need to use our minds and make decisions that are based on current information. Basic moral principles of the gospel of Jesus Christ never change, but practices and implementation do—or why would we have continuous revelation? Some of us have a hard time embracing changes that are probably planned. We spend some good todays struggling with pain as we try to correlate the past with today.

President Kimball takes every opportunity to tell others that his Camilla has never stopped learning—how, in fact, she took classes each year at the University of Utah or at the institute of religion on that campus.

Our mind is an amazing thing. President Jeffrey R. Holland says, "What the mind can conceive and believe, it can achieve." The famous psychologist William James said, "Be careful what you expect. You will probably get it."

In an Education Week talk at the Institute of Religion at the University of Utah, Sister Leisel McBride told the following story as it was reported in a Chicago paper: One Friday afternoon a man found himself locked in a refrigerator car. He called until he was hoarse. He banged on the well-insulated walls. At last he realized that working hours were over until Monday morning. He sat huddled in a corner or scrawled his thoughts on the walls with his pencil. One sentence was weakly written and the words slanted off at an angle. It said, "I am slowly freezing to death. These words will probably be the last I write." On Monday morning his fellow workers found their associate in a corner, and he was, indeed, lifeless. The unusual circumstance was that the refrigeration in that car had been turned off on Friday, and there was only a normal, livable temperature in the car.

If a mind can snuff out a life, surely, if properly used, it can also help bring the abundant life. When we learn how to use such a powerful tool to solve our own problems and help with our progress, the effect can be exhilarating. We cheat ourselves when we rationalize or place the blame for our circumstances on someone else. Somehow we would all like excuses for our mistakes, our lack of happiness, or our slow progress.

Have you ever heard, "I'm like this because I'm the middle child," or "I came from the wrong side of the tracks," or "My boss doesn't like me," or "My husband just doesn't understand," or "I'm naturally shy"? Others may be responsible in the beginning for some of our problems, but they are not responsible for the way we act or the way we solve our problems. Learning to cope with all phases of life is an important part of the learning process.

Dr. Sterling G. Ellsworth and Dr. Richard G. Ellsworth, in their book *Getting to Know the Real You* (Deseret Book, 1980), tell the following story. Two girls were standing in the hall at high school. They were not attractive. They had large noses and braces on their teeth. As they stood there, along came the captain of the football team. He had an inflated ego and was aggressive and superficially confident. He looked at the two girls and said, "You girls are really ugly. You are bad news. Why don't you get lost?" He sauntered down the hall and then looked back. One girl burst into tears, and he laughed. But the other girl looked him right in the eye and said, "Buddy, *you* have the problem, not I. You must have had a fight with your mother, or something. What are you doing going around at eight-thirty in the morning telling other people that they are bad news? What is the matter with *you?*" This girl was secure. She had learned of her intrinsic worth. The other girl let someone else crush her. Her whole day was probably ruined.

Our egos are fragile and easily wounded. However, our minds are tools that can teach us that as others attack us, say unkind words, ignore us, or hurt us in any way, they are the ones who are hurting and insecure. This is a hard lesson to learn, but if we can learn it we won't waste beautiful todays in tears and hurt feelings.

There is another art to be learned to make each day easier. Decisions, decisions, decisions. I really don't know how one learns to make them quickly, but I do know that I can waste a lot of time on a good day agonizing over a proper menu for a dinner party or what kind of gift I should give someone special.

A great banker said that the secret to his success was following this advice: "When you have a decision to make, make it and go ahead. You will make some mistakes; but you will make no more mistakes than if you took a month to decide, and you will have thirty days where you didn't have to worry about it."

The story of Zode, as told by Dr. Seuss, puts a humorous light on this problem. Zode came to a fork in the road and couldn't decide which road to take, no matter how he pondered. So he decided to take both, and he started off for both places at once. And that is how he ended up—no place at all with a split in his pants. Prompt decision-making can make a day brighter.

There are so many dimensions of learning, so much our minds can do. President J. Reuben Clark said, "All domains of knowledge belong to us. In no other way could the great law of eternal progress be satisfied."

After spending full time with her husband for the four months after his surgery, Sister Kimball finally joined the General Authorities' wives at our monthly luncheon. She was asked to say a few words to us. In four months, she told us, she had been out in public only four times—having spent each day by her husband's side—yet there was never a word of complaint. Instead, she said, "I have learned that every experience in life is a learning experience. During these last few months I have learned so much. I have become aware that one is never above learning nor too old to learn."

From her we can learn that when sorrow and tragedy come into our lives, it is normal to react with tears and anguish. But if we have learned to trust in God, we won't be paralyzed by these feelings, and we can move forward and often experience "the peace . . . which passeth all understanding." (Philippians 4:7.) As we learn of God's ways and grow through testing, our troubled days can be good days, learning days. Theodore Rubin said, "Happiness is found more frequently in times of struggle than in times of triumph." Even in trials and sorrow, learning can take place. Without the benefit of constant learning, our todays become stagnant, our lives out of date, and our progress limited.

All the loving and all the learning are then put to the test as we live day by day. What shall I do? What shall I leave undone? After whom shall I pattern my life? How shall I dress? For whom shall I vote? Where shall I go to school? How should I act? Actually, we must find our own answers. So many of us would like a church program or policy outlined for every contingency in our lives. Then we wouldn't have to reason it out for ourselves. When we made a mistake or experienced a failure, we could shrug our shoulders and say, "It's not my fault. I only followed the manual." That would be the easy way, but not the growing way. As the Lord told Oliver Cowdery, "Behold, ye have not understood; you have supposed that I would give it unto you, when you took no thought save it was to ask me." (D&C 9:7.)

Sometimes two right principles do conflict. Our agency is given to us to decide what is right for us at this moment. Satisfaction comes as we solve our own problems, using gospel guidelines while we exercise our agency. All of us have stood at the crossroads and doubted our wisdom to choose the right path. It is our right and our responsibility to determine what is best for us at any given time. As we do so, may we use our power to decide and to live with our decisions, without being ridden with guilt.

At times we choose to do some things well, leave some things undone, or do some things not so well so we can hurry on to more important tasks. "Ought to's" and "shoulds" are usually not commandments. Do you ever feel as though you have broken a commandment when you haven't gotten all the "shoulds" done? (A "should" is unhealthy only when it gets in the way of healthy, effective behavior.) "Ought to's" and "shoulds" shouldn't get bigger than we are.

President Stone of the Modesto California Stake told us that his wife felt she should always serve home-baked bread to him and their eight children. He loved the bread and so did the children, but one day he banned homemade bread from their table. He helped his wife realize that there were more important things at that time in her life than homemade bread. She needed more time for him and for herself. It was one thing that helped her be less tired.

Can you give away a bushel of peaches instead of canning them if your husband wants you to go on a date with him? Can you choose to take a class instead of sewing all your children's clothes and not feel guilty when your neighbor's children march into church in their home-sewn dresses? On some days can you throw the covers up quickly on the bed so you can hurry off to play tennis because you decide you need exercise more than a perfectly made bed? Can you use your agency in these seemingly insignificant ways without feeling weighed down with guilt? If so, you are living well today.

In daily living, self-judgment and guilt can ruin a day or many days. Some around us may flaunt their spiritual blessings as they talk of children who filled missions, who had temple marriages, and who are models in every way. And as we listen, we judge ourselves as failures. I once heard my husband suggest that such a father should go to his closet and thank his Father in heaven very often, but also consider how he might make some who weren't so fortunate feel when he talked of his model family.

The size of a family, conduct of children, positions held may be indicators, but they don't necessarily determine our status in the eyes of God. In fact, who is to say that the parents who go on loving and trying to help a wayward child through long years or the women with no children who teach, serve, and live with quiet dignity will not have a greater reward than those who are fortunate enough to have a model family? I somehow think they will.

Enjoyable days come from enjoying and working with what we have today instead of yearning for different circumstances. Often there is a great desire to look to tomorrow, to "jump out of season." The young person who drives before the legal time; the student who is bored with school and, wanting spending money, drops out to get a job that pays minimum wages; starry-eyed couples who mistake infatuation and physical attraction for enduring love and rush to the altar—these and so many others jump out of season.

A young mother with several children decided that it was the season for genealogy work. While her children ran around the neighborhood, rather neglected, her genealogy sheets covered the floors and tables of her home. When a friend came to call and saw the state of affairs, she asked why this woman spent all her time with her ancestors and so little time with her children. The genealogist thought for a moment and then answered, "I guess it is because I can get along with the dead better than with the living."

Another mother was so anxious to get back to school that she left several teenagers to fend for themselves. Today that woman has her doctorate, but most of her children are in serious trouble with drugs and the law. Education is wonderful, as is genealogy, but there is the right season for them. Even though out-of-season activities may beckon enticingly, they usually bring on some stressful todays. Remember, results of unwise actions are often not evident until after the fact. I hope that we won't jump forward or backward out of season and miss the season of life in which we find ourselves. I believe that happiness comes when we allow ourselves to grow according to the season in which we find ourselves planted today. Spiritual experiences usually come as we do our routine tasks following gospel guidelines.

There are many more aspects of living than we have touched on today. Examine your own life. See where stress is causing uncomfortable todays; then move to correct the situation. Seek help, if necessary. No one is perfect, even if you have a neighbor you might think is a supermom. There is no such person.

All of us hope to reach some magical goal where our job is recognized as well done and our just rewards will be bestowed upon us. But especially as Latter-day Saints, we need to remember that our goal is eternal progression and that there is no such end of the journey. Therefore, if we haven't enjoyed ourselves along the way, we have missed the only joy there really is.

As the threads of the gospel weave back and forth through our daily living, unexpected joys and sometimes miracles will enrich our lives. Testimonies can grow stronger. I like the story found in the ninth chapter of Mark, where the father brought his sick son to the disciples of Jesus to be healed, but they failed to heal him. The father lost hope. Then came Jesus, who said, "If thou canst believe, all things are possible to him that believeth." The father answered, "Lord, I believe." And the son was healed. (See Mark 9:15-29.)

If we can believe, our days can go from joy to joy.

General Douglas MacArthur wrote, "People grow old only by deserting their ideals. Years may wrinkle the skin, but to give up wrinkles the soul. You are as young as your faith, as old as your doubts; as young as your self-confidence, as old as your fears; as young as your hopes, as old as your despairs." To me he is saying we should love and learn and live each day that is ours to live. "For behold, this life is the time for men to prepare to meet God; yea, behold, the day of this life is the day for men to perform their labors." (Alma 34:32.) Your own expectations are the key. If you expect to be happy and fulfilled in life, most likely that is what will happen.

In a shopping mall the other day, a tall, good-looking youth walked toward me. When he got close enough, I could read these words on the front of his T-shirt: "I'd try having a positive mental attitude." As he moved on past me, I saw these words on the back of the shirt: "But I know it won't work."

I promise you that the daily enjoyment of life does work if you work on it and want it to. Love yourself and all of God's children. Appreciate your innate nobility. Take charge of your own life by using your agency wisely and without guilt feelings. Be your own best self, not a carbon copy. Stay pliable by reaching into the great fountains of knowledge offered both in secular areas and in gospel teachings. Then joy can be yours all along the way, and the nows will be more rewarding than the dreams of tomorrow.

Norma B. Ashton graduated in elementary education and English from the University of Utah. She has given extensive service to the Church and the community. She is married to Elder Marvin J. Ashton, a member of the Council of the Twelve Apostles.

Blueprints for Living

BARBARA B. SMITH

ecently I have been made very much aware of what goes into the development of a blueprint. My daughter and her husband have just decided to build a home. They are in the process of selecting and planning—blueprinting, if you will. Let me review with you what I have observed in their exciting new venture.

First, they began by looking around for a lot, surveying all the available land in a location suitable for their needs. Then, when they finally found what to them was the perfect place for their house, they had it appraised and surveyed. Next, they purchased the property. Then came hours and hours of talking and intently planning together to identify the things they both wanted in their dream home. What style should it be: French, English Tudor, colonial, a ranch-type rambler? What general floor plan should they choose: one level or two? What kind of room requirements: a family room and dining room, and of course a kitchen and bedrooms, but how many, and where should they be located? And how many baths? With five children, a clothes chute into the laundry room was a must. What extras could they afford within their budget? A spiral staircase? built-in, rotating storage shelves? a fireplace.

What special needs does each member of the family have? What are their needs, individually and collectively: a stereo cabinet for one child, full-length mirrors for another, study areas?

They began to consider how they wanted the house finished. Of what material should it be made: brick, wood, stone? Or should they use some of the new and different sidings currently available? What colors? Earth tones and pastels are good now. And furnishings: period, modern, or early American?

They spent hours putting down on paper their ideas, needs, and wants; then they sought the services of a good architect who could take their roughly sketched ideas, refine them, and translate them into a blueprint. The blueprint is then to be professionally drawn with exact detail so that it can be given to a builder who will be able to estimate the cost, materials, and skilled craftsmen necessary to make that plan a reality.

Well, my children are just in the beginning of this process, and I recognize that there are still so many fundamental and important decisions for them to make that it will be quite some time before they finally have a new home. But as I thought about them and the years ahead, and reviewed the process of building, I was forcibly struck by the parallel between the process of building a home, which they are in, and the process of building a life, which you are in.

Let us focus our attention on four similarities:
1. Selecting our lot in life.
2. Building our life's foundation.
3. Constructing a framework for all we do.
4. Finishing the structure by becoming what we want some day to be.

The first step I mentioned, selecting the lot, surveying the land, and making related choices, begins early in life; and as you approach adulthood, you have the responsibility of assuming the control and direction of your own life. In the decisions of adolescence, we begin to look around us and form impressions of the world in which we live. Often we experience terrible growing pains as we have certain experiences. Some we choose, and others are thrust upon us by our parents, our peers, or circumstances.

Regardless of circumstances, you must ultimately decide what kind of a human being you are going to be, upon what philosophies you are going to build your life, and what style of life you will live. Will your choices be based upon worldly or spiritual values?

What attitudes toward the experiences of mortality will you develop? Do you favor the cool, noncommital way of breezing past events, or do you like a negative, pessimistic outlook, or, possibly, do you prefer a happy, optimistic attitude? I often think of a friend who smiled the moment she awoke. "I love to open my eyes to each new day," she confessed. There was optimism and enthusiasm in her approach—an attitude she *chose* to have.

What will you do with your life in your day-to-day living? How will you relate to the members of your family and your neighbors? Will you volunteer yourself to reach out to someone, or will you shut your eyes to everyone outside your own little circle?

What general scheme of planning will you adopt—a daily organized routine requiring self-discipline, or will you just let things come as they may?

Where will you stand in relationship to God? Will you have a program of daily prayer and meditation, will you become a scholar of the scriptures, or will you find yourself too busy to read? Will you choose to serve the Lord, or will you just wait and see what happens?

What kind of time are you willing to give, and what kind of planning for a lifetime of education, training, and continual growth do you want?

Experts who study human behavior point out that there is a great need for making a lifetime plan, realistically recognizing what each period of life is likely to bring. Alena H. Moris, president of Seattle's Individual Development Center, points out: "With some kind of a good design to life rather than a random existence which does not give security, one can lead a life that is potent and dynamic, one that provides all of the satisfaction of

knowing that you are becoming what you are capable of being."
(*Deseret News,* April 10, 1979.)

Childhood is a special time. It is one of enormous growth and development. I remember my mother once said, "Spend all the time you possibly can with your children; they will grow up so fast and leave your home that you will hardly know it is happening." I thought, "Mother, you've forgotten how long the time is when you are so hard at work with and for them." Now I know she was right. Like it or not, believe it or not, children do grow up all too quickly; and, in large measure, they reach out and participate in the excitement of learning only when it is encouraged and nurtured in their home and in the larger environment in which those early years are spent.

Can there be any wonder at the vital importance of the home when we realize the profound effect these early years have upon the lives of children? It is in the home that the life of a child is primarily shaped. The home is also the significant factor in determining the existence, or the nonexistence, of the basic problems in society, such as divorce, crime, suicide, and all manner of social disorders.

After childhood comes the period of choice and preparation. That is where most of you are now, surveying the fields of interest, taking classes, and focusing attention on understanding and developing your personal interests and talents. I hope you realize that your potential for study and the opportunity to develop new educational skills will probably never again be quite as available to you as they are now. In this springtime of your life you should concentrate on learning and preparing yourself with professional skills, with a single-mindedness that may never be possible again.

I believe that one never gets too much education. In fact, one great principle of the gospel teaches us that we need to commit ourselves to a lifetime of continuous learning, and I think that learning needs to include ways of applying in practical ways newly acquired information.

This period of your life is the time to upgrade your marketable skills, for no one knows when or where a woman might be called upon to provide the money to support herself. Elder

Howard W. Hunter stated it insightfully when he said: "There are impelling reasons for our sisters to plan toward employment also. We want them to obtain all the education and vocational training possible before marriage. If they become widowed or divorced and have to work, we want them to have dignified and rewarding employment. If a sister does not marry, she has every right to engage in a profession that allows her to magnify her talent and gifts." ("Prepare for Honorable Employment," *Ensign,* November 1975, p. 124.)

Your surveying should include selecting a mate, one with whom you can share the world's experiences and one with whom you will be able to build an eternal companionship. This selection is the single most important decision you will ever make. Upon this choice depends your mortal and eternal relationships. It will determine how you care for the children you bear and how they will increase in stature, in wisdom, and in favor with God and man. And it will determine your growth in these ways also.

Then, looking way down the road, what happens when your children are grown and off in pursuit of their own interests? Where will you spend your time so that you can make the most of that season of your life?

All of this is but a part of that important process of selecting your lot. Land is not always what it seems to be on the surface. A careful builder always has a contour map made before his work actually begins. He needs to know what kind of underground water is present. Are there huge boulders under the surface? What is the composition of the soil?

Remember that in living your life, you too must consider the lay of the land. The Lord has counseled: "Therefore whosoever heareth these sayings of mine, and doeth them, I will liken him unto a wise man, which built his house upon a rock: and the rain descended, and the floods came, and the winds blew, and beat upon that house; and it fell not: for it was founded upon a rock. And every one that heareth these sayings of mine, and doeth them not, shall be likened unto a foolish man, which built his house upon the sand: and the rain descended, and the floods came, and the winds blew, and beat

upon that house; and it fell: and great was the fall of it."
(Matthew 7:24-27.)

No structure can stand long upon land that is faulty. Sandy
soil will wash away, and no matter how strong the structure
upon it, that building will be destroyed. So it is with all of us. If
we choose to live in shaky, immoral environments, we have to
recognize that the nature of the soil upon which we build will
bring about our destruction.

After the lot is properly chosen and prepared, then the
builder begins. He takes great care in preparing and pouring
the foundation because he knows that a good, well-engineered
foundation is critical.

Revelation from the Lord is the great foundation stone of all
happy, productive living. He is the source of all truth and re-
liable knowledge. He has given us an open invitation to come to
him for information, for direction, and for rest in times of trials
and tribulations. A personal relationship to God is essential for
a firm foundation.

You need to know how the mortal and the immortal fit together. You need to know how heaven and earth interrelate.
You need to know that you can communicate individually with
your Heavenly Father.

How do you come to such truth? The blueprints that the
Lord has provided—the holy scriptures—tell you to use profoundly practical steps if you wish to know. You might think of it
in scientific terms: formulate a hypothesis, act upon that
hypothesis, evaluate the results of the experiment, and then
reevaluate the hypothesis in the light of the new information.

How could that work with the gospel? Well, you make an
informed observation, your hypothesis. For instance: God lives.
Then you begin to live according to that hypothesis. Study the
scriptures, and read as Joseph Smith did: "If any of you lack
wisdom, let him ask of God, that giveth to all men liberally, and
upbraideth not. . . . But let him ask in faith, nothing wavering."
(James 1:5-6.) And the truth will be manifest unto you.

In Matthew 7:7 we read: "Ask, and it shall be given you; seek,
and ye shall find; knock, and it shall be opened unto you." This

invitation to the most profoundly important information in the world is repeated over and over again in the scriptures. In fact, in the *Topical Guide to the Scriptures,* "Knock, and it shall be opened unto you" is listed as appearing thirteen times in the Bible, the Book of Mormon, and the Doctrine and Covenants. It seems to be a very important detail in the blueprint for living. It is repeated carefully, simply, completely, and often. Listen to the way the Savior expresses it in Revelation 3:20: "Behold, I stand at the door, and knock: if any man hear my voice, and open the door, I will come in to him, and will sup with him, and he with me."

The fundamental unity of Latter-day Saint women comes from the one thing that each of us can have: a testimony of an eternal plan of life and salvation; the testimony that God lives; the testimony that we are his children and that we individually have access to the powers of heaven; and a testimony that we are led by his prophet here upon the earth today.

The journals of the early Mormon women of this dispensation tell us that they were seeking light and truth, and they could not find satisfaction in their souls that what they had was enough. Then they heard about Joseph Smith, or they heard about the golden plates, or an elder came knocking at their doors and told them the truth had been restored. They asked the Lord if what they were hearing was true, and light came into their lives. The witness of the Holy Spirit was like a light being turned on in their souls. They would not and could not be persuaded otherwise.

Sister Eliza R. Snow says that her father, in assisting widows and others, was detained until the very last day of grace allotted to the Mormons for leaving the county; the weather was very cold indeed, and the ground was covered with snow. She walked on to warm her aching feet until the teams would overtake her; meanwhile she met one of the so-called militia, who abruptly accosted her: "Well, I think this will cure you of your faith." The young heroine looked him steadily in the eye and replied: "It will take more than this to cure me of my faith." His countenance fell, and he responded, "I must confess you are a better soldier than I am." (Shirley Anderson Cazier, comp. and ed., "Eliza R. Snow, as Seen through the Woman's Exponent 1872-87," unpublished manuscript.)

These sisters had a personal witness that the gospel was restored and that they could become part of building this kingdom of God on earth, which would then take that glad message throughout the world. I suppose the poet captured the feelings of their quest and the personal nature of this foundation when he declared: "Back into the heart's small house I crept and fell upon my knees and wept, and lo, He came to me." (Author Unknown.)

If you remember nothing more of what I say today, I pray you will hear my own testimony and act upon this one truth. The strongest, firmest, most sure foundation for your life is a personal testimony of the truth that God lives, that he speaks again to us, and that he cares for each of us. This testimony will come to you if you will ask in faith, nothing wavering, and with sincere intent. My dear sisters, millions have a testimony, and it can be yours also if you will but ask the Lord in constant, secret prayer.

Regarding the third step, any good house blueprint calls for a strong framework upon which to build. And so it is with life. The individual needs to construct a strong framework upon which to build. In building a house, one selects good, firm timbers or strong, tempered steel that can bear the weight of the rest of the structure and withstand the ravages of weather and natural disaster.

In building a life, a person needs to choose good, strong tenets and assemble them into a design that gives stability and unity and yet allows for the constant addition of new information and further insights. This is the essence of gospel teaching.

The blueprint from the Lord suggests the need to build our lives using two fundamental principles.

The first is the personal quest for eternal perfection, achieved line upon line, precept upon precept, with each new insight giving us greater vision. When we seek to be constantly improving, overcoming faults and weaknesses, and searching for enriching, enlarging opportunities, life becomes full of meaningful experiences. Remember that perfection is a process, not a state we achieve. We are continually involved in learning today what will give us the information and experience we need for tomorrow.

The second fundamental principle is that we should give service to and perform acts of compassionate care for others throughout our lives, for doing so allows us to develop Godlike attributes.

Holding the framework securely together, and essential to every addition, is charity. According to the scriptures, without charity all else is as "sounding brass, or a tinkling cymbal." (1 Corinthians 13:1.) Charity is the pure love of Christ—everlasting love—and unless we have charity, we cannot be saved. Further, we are shown in the Lord's blueprint that we should have charity for all, even those who despitefully use us, and that without charity, all that we do is of no value.

If you choose this sound, basic structure, you will have a life with endless potential. You will be able to spend your lifetime finishing the structure—completing it, furnishing it, and enriching it. That is why it is important to have a good blueprint. Make your plans with such care that the structure will stand firm and unshakable. Then imaginatively and creatively go forward with the finish work of your house.

You can prioritize the items you want to add until the structure is complete. In your day-to-day living, that means beginning to develop within yourself the attributes that make you the kind of person you want to be. You might begin by developing your talents. You have special gifts, and the Lord expects you to develop them fully and then use them to build his kingdom here on earth. You might begin by increasing your knowledge, or you might choose to begin by giving service.

When you begin may not be nearly so important as that you do begin. The gospel provides a vision of your fulfillment as a woman, an understanding of your future as an eternally oriented human being—a woman who is strong, competent, and filled with capabilities and commitment to a quest that will keep you constantly achieving.

I am sure you feel grateful, as I do, that you need not be

fearful of life, for the Savior came to show the way and to conquer death. His atonement made possible your salvation and exaltation.

So if you are willing to accept the gospel blueprint and adapt the framework design to your own life, you can move forward, encouraged to finish your unique structure by developing all of your talents. You will look to the future with enthusiasm and hope, for the Lord has removed the pain of death and has taught that even errors are to be viewed as learning experiences.

Nothing that is for your good is forbidden, but cautionary signs do warn of those things that bring sorrow and unhappiness. Basically, this mortal experience is to give you a variety of situations in which you can test yourself and develop the qualities that will make you worthy to return again and dwell with Him who made us.

Perhaps even more basic is the realization that you should be developing the attitudes and character traits that will make you capable of eternal progression. Such is your birthright. The capabilities and powers are within you, and you must live to bring them forth.

When builders are working on a new structure, and the threat of bad weather comes or winter approaches, they quickly work to close things in. I've heard at least two reasons for this. First, good builders want to get the outer shell completed so that they can work throughout the storms to complete the inside of the building. Second, they want to protect the interior from the ravages of bad weather because usually the materials that are needed in finishing the structure are not designed to withstand the elements in the same way as those on the outside. The finishing work needed to complete a life is somewhat the same.

I do not offer these suggestions as a matter of preferential priority, but I do suggest that both exterior and interior finish work are necessary. In fact, the finishing work in building a life is never completed. It goes on throughout mortality and throughout eternity. Change from the outside will occur just as surely as the sun rises and sets. Change from the inside will likewise occur—for the worse if we just drift, for the better if we determine to work to achieve goals. Transferring general ideas onto a blueprint and then transforming the drawings into reality requires many carefully detailed tasks and countless thoughtful decisions. It is the work of a lifetime.

In looking to the exterior finishing, be aware of the great variety of exteriors available. No two women look exactly alike. It was never the intent of the Lord that they should, but he enjoins us to know and understand the workings of our bodies and thereby to comprehend what helps and what hurts their functions.

A healthy body is more pleasing to look at and its movements are more graceful, thus affording the benefits of both looking and feeling better. One of the Relief Society board members strives for a physically fit body by jogging in her room and memorizing scriptures at the same time, surely a pleasing combination.

The adornment of the human body is another point of exterior finish. It involves what you wear, your makeup, your jewelry, your grooming habits, your style preferences. Brigham Young told the people there was reason to believe that the angels of heaven were lovely to look upon. He encouraged the sisters to be neat and clean and beautiful. He also felt strongly that fashion excesses were to be avoided. That kind of balance should still concern us.

We should all keep ourselves neat and clean. Most of us can do this. Some time spent in making ourselves attractive is important, for it makes us feel better and helps other people feel better about us.

There is wisdom in developing one's sense of style. I once knew a young, attractive buyer in a large department store. She gave a talk to some blind women, at their request, about fashion and style. They had invited her to come to a meeting they held regularly for the purpose of helping them improve their looks.

She sat in that room as the preliminaries were being handled and looked at these well-dressed, sightless women. I don't know what thoughts went through her mind, for she was a woman trained in and sensitive to the visual line and color of ready-made dresses and coats. But when she stood up and talked, she explained to them the one thing that was the most useful for them to know. I have thought about this many times since, and I believe it is the most useful single thing for any of us to know about clothes.

"Fashion," she said, "has to do with fad and style. That which is high fashion is often faddish in nature. It will be good for a short season, and then it will be gone. Style, on the other hand, is the fashion line that is classic in nature. It will always be in good taste, with perhaps minor alterations now and then."

So a person can be well dressed by paying close attention to the purchase of a dress with a style that will have a long life and by paying only casual attention to the faddish elements of the new season.

This same effort to develop good taste in makeup, hair styling, grooming of any kind, shoes, dresses, coats, jackets, and clothing of all kinds will make it possible for us to be attractive on the outside.

I think it is important to be mindful of the cautions given in the past that we not become slaves to appearance and that we not put undue emphasis on externals. Nevertheless, how we look is important. Costume designers for dramatic productions spend their lives studying and trying to understand the language of external human appearances. And these appearances are very clever. They can create a mood; they can tell us something about a person's experiences in life; they can even tell us about a person's attitudes.

Sometimes on the stage, as in life, a costume will give insight into a person's character and feeling. A very dramatic example of this occurs in the play *The Prime of Miss Jean Brodie*. Miss Brodie is a flamboyant teacher of young girls who has dedicated her life to molding and shaping the minds and characters of her charges. She is very romantic and a little unrealistic. The colors and the fabrics used for Miss Brodie's costumes visually portray these facets of her character in the scene in which she comes into conflict with the headmistress. At the moment of dismissal from her position, she pulls on a gray coat, and as the top button is closed, the gray covers all of the vibrant, romantic color, and we see the transformation of Miss Brodie. The color and the line of the coat subtly reinforce the pathos of the play.

It is very unrealistic to assume that the clothes we wear and the appearance we are satisfied with have no effect upon the course of our lives. They do. We all respond to the visual appearance of people and to our own appearance. We must make personal decisions about our exterior finish.

Another aspect of this exterior finish is the matter of manners—our social behavior patterns, our attitudes, and the effect they have upon our relationships with others.

Think about the endless detail found in the variety of patterns that our associations generate. We live in a world of constant change. The most constant thing of all is the continuing change in human relationships. The world of people is like a giant kaleidoscope. A twist, a turn, or even a bump, and the relationships of human beings to each other change and move; another forward or reverse turn and the relationships change again. It's a very exciting, worrisome, satisfying, puzzling, challenging world in which we live.

I would not like to leave with you the impression that appearances and external relationships are so important as to justify spending all of your time with them. They are not, and you must use restraint and good judgment so that you do not waste precious time or become vain. What I do want to point out is that your exterior finish does influence your life. It invites people to you and to some extent governs their attitudes toward you. It is also true that what you wear, how you look, and how you think about yourself influence how you feel.

In the film *West Side Story,* Maria first discovers her feelings of love as she sings, "I feel pretty, oh so pretty." Of course, it is proverbial that a woman in love looks beautiful.

A stage designer I know once conducted a workshop for the Church. As he was teaching the volunteers how to make costumes, some wanted to use a shortcut and hem the period skirts by machine. Painstakingly, he explained that hand-stitched hems look better because they flow and move more easily. "That's important on the stage," he said, "because it helps the actress. If she feels that she looks graceful, she will perform better."

This is the reason I mention outward appearances and manners today. They are necessary to complete your life. The exterior finish of the house is what invites us in.

But of far greater significance is the finish on the inside. On the inside lies true beauty. On the inside lies the motivation for all that we do. You can select and polish those characteristics for which you wish to be known. Will you be honest? Will you be chaste? Will you be kind? Will you have integrity?

You and I alone determine the interior finish of our souls. The choices we make individually are the ones that ultimately set in place the furnishings.

Will you be part of the creative force that allows human life to continue on this earth? Only your personal decisions concerning the bearing of children, if you have a choice, can determine that. Will you be part of the rearing of children? Only your decisions and actions can determine that. Will you marry if a mutually satisfying opportunity comes your way? Only you can decide that.

Will you be lonely in this life? Probably. Everybody knows some loneliness. But will your loneliness engulf you and stop your progress? Only you can decide that. Single or married, you will have times of choice in your life. Will you seek out opportunities to give love or won't you? Only you can decide, but upon that decision so much else depends. One thing is certain, though: if you give love to all you encounter—and if you seek opportunities to give love to those who hunger and thirst and have great need—then love will flow back to you, and you will not be alone.

So it goes, down the whole catalog of human characteristics. Which ones do you wish to have? Which ones are you willing to cultivate and develop? The interior finish of your life depends upon such decisions.

One of the great teachings of the restored gospel is that each person has the right and the responsibility to determine the direction of his or her life. So it is with each of you. So it is with me.

The English writer Somerset Maugham, who was known as a great cynic, once wrote a book called *Summing Up.* In this volume he described each of the Christian virtues and put them down one by one as being full of fraud or hypocrisy. Then he came toward the end of the book, and he wrote that, despite his disillusionment with these so-called virtues, when he found himself in the presence of a truly good person, his heart knelt in reverence.

So finish your structure with the characteristics of faith, hope, and charity, remembering that the greatest of these is charity. Seek wisdom and give service freely. In these ways you will adorn your life with the beauties that radiate from within.

Circumstances and opportunities vary for each person. You have to seek out those opportunities that will allow *you* to develop, and you must be responsible for the choices you make as well as the consequences of those choices for yourself, for others, and for society in general.

The Lord requires only that you do the best you can to gain experience and that you continue your growth by participating with a willing heart and teachable spirit.

Think often:

> The beauty of the house is order;
> The blessing of the house is contentment;
> The glory of the house is hospitality;
> The crown of the house is godliness.

I testify that you will have order, contentment, hospitality, and godliness as you build your life according to an eternal blueprint.

Barbara B. Smith served as general president of the Relief Society from October 1974 to April 1984. She was also chairman of the Childhood and Family Committee of the National Council of Women and a member of the Brigham Young University Board of Trustees.

A Woman's Role and Destiny

IDA SMITH

Over one hundred and fifty years ago the Lord restored the gospel of Jesus Christ to the earth through the boy prophet, Joseph Smith. Through this young man, knowledge and information that had been lost, forgotten, changed, and, in some cases, denied, for nineteen centuries was once again made available to the children of God. In most cases the inhabitants of the earth were no more ready to receive the gospel in 1830 than they had been to receive it from the Savior himself nineteen hundred years before. As the Prophet described it, the vision and understanding of the people suffered because of the "traditions of their fathers"—and, I would add, because of their mothers, as well.

The people cried blasphemy when the Prophet declared that not only could God still talk to man (revelation had not ceased), but that he *had* talked to him. He was denounced when he claimed that God and Christ had corporeal bodies—separate, distinct, and tangible.

But this was only the beginning of new, revealed truths to come to the world through this young prophet chosen to usher in the last dispensation. And history shows that the world at large was still not ready, able, or willing to receive most of what he taught.

From a tiny core of devoted converts, the Lord sent out missionaries to preach the restored gospel, and as the little band of "Mormons" grew, the Prophet Joseph endeavored to teach and prepare a Zion people that could, one day, teach and bless the Lord's children all over the world. Many of the revealed truths found unpalatable then still stick in some throats today; but one area of knowledge—hard, if not impossible, to swallow then—is finally, in our day, coming into its own. That area: Women.

The Prophet Joseph Smith did more than just preach that men and women were of equal value and importance in the sight of God. He preached that in order for a man to achieve his highest potential (the celestial kingdom and godhood), he must have a woman—equally exalted—by his side and sealed to him forever. (See D&C 131:1-2; 132:4.) A just God would not require the yoking of two unequal beings for eternity. Joseph also learned that our Father in heaven is not single, that we have a mother in heaven as well, that together they reign, and that we are made in their image—male and female.

As temples were built and temple ordinances restored, our knowledge of the eternal values of the male-female relationship has increased. We now know that both men and women share in *all* the blessings of the priesthood and that both share in all the gifts of the spirit (i.e., to heal, to be healed, to speak in tongues, to prophesy, etc.). We now know that the man's function in the priesthood is to administer, that the woman's function is creative, and that together they have a perfect balance. As Paul stated, "Neither is the man without the woman, neither the woman without the man, in the Lord." (1 Corinthians 11:11.)

Marriage may or may not happen during our stay in the second estate. President Kimball said in his talk to women in September 1979: "Sometimes to be tested and proved requires that we be temporarily deprived—but righteous women and men will one day receive *all* that our Father has. It is not only worth waiting for—it is worth living for! Meanwhile, one does not need to be married or a mother in order to keep the first and second great commandments—to love God and our fellowmen—on which, Jesus said, hang all the law and all the prophets." (*My Beloved Sisters,* Deseret Book, 1979, p. 41.)

The important thing for a woman to learn in this life is her eternal role so that when she is sealed, she will be prepared and ready—with all her heart—to function in and glorify that role. That means being ready and prepared to function as a full partner in a celestial team—without having to look *up* for help and direction or look *down* because of any feeling of superiority, but being able to look *across* into the eyes of an equally prepared, equally magnificent eternal mate.

Such an exalted role for women was mind-boggling for nineteenth-century America. Here, as elsewhere, not only were most societies male-dominated, but men were generally regarded as superior beings. Men were not only to be protectors of women, but they were responsible for the salvation of women as well.

When the Prophet Joseph organized the women after the pattern of the priesthood in 1842, he charged them that from that time forth, they were responsible for their own sins. This was a radical thought in those days. He taught them that they were responsible for their own salvation, that they had access to every blessing the priesthood had access to, that they had equal access to the Holy Ghost and to every spiritual gift, that they also had direct access to the Savior—to model him, to become like him, to be heirs in his kingdom.

The Prophet removed some of the excuses afforded woman in her passive, dependent role and made her responsible for herself. In a very real way, he started the modern-day women's movement. Many of the early Mormon sisters caught his vision for women, got in the game, and ran with the ball. Women in Utah and Wyoming had the vote fifty years before women in the United States received it generally. And as we read and ponder the writings of many nineteenth-century Latter-day Saint women, we know that they knew who they were.

Somewhere in the last eighty or so years, Mormon women have not only dropped the ball, but they have left the game. And as we have watched from the sidelines the growth of the women's movement in the hands of the world, we have been aghast at some of its excesses and some of the directions it has taken. It is the devil's pattern to imitate God's plan and to thereby deceive mankind. Whereas God wants us to know that we are of equal value and importance, the devil would have us believe that we are not different, but the same. The Lord's way is to become like each other only as we take upon ourselves *all* of the Savior's traits; the devil's way would be for us to become a unisex society. We must be careful not to confuse the phony with the real thing.

Some women complain that they have no strong role models in the scriptures. That is not true, for we have many. And our main model is the same as for men—the Savior. Nowhere is it written that he is a model for men only; nowhere is it written that he came to save men only; nowhere is it written that men and women should each be allowed only half of his traits. The world has divided up character and personality traits and has labeled some of them masculine and some of them feminine. Latter-day Saints—of all people in the world—should know better than to be deceived by this. Nowhere does the Lord say that tenderness, kindness, charity, faithfulness, patience, gentleness, and compassion are female traits and should be exemplified by women only. And nowhere does he say that courage, strength, determination, leadership, and a willingness to fight—and, if necessary, die—for what is right should be the exclusive prerogatives of men. Any notion that God desires that women should remain passive bystanders should have been dispelled when the Prophet told women they are, from 1842 forward, responsible for their own salvation.

Not just women suffer with sexual categorization; man is also charged to become Christlike. A heavy burden is placed on him when he realizes that many of the traits that will make him Christlike have been labeled by the world as feminine, and that by taking upon himself those characteristics, he will run the risk of having his masculinity seriously questioned by his peers. In the world, in most societies throughout history, masculinity has been equated with virility, or, in today's vernacular, *macho* behavior. Women have usually been considered seductive and submissive. The world, unwilling to admit the Creation, has tried to explain existence and behavior as physical and has succumbed to the process of fragmenting the whole person.

As members of the Church, we find ourselves running from the present movement—which would give human beings back their wholeness—for fear of moving into a unisex society. And we are justified in running because that's the imitation. The Lord's plan is for men and women to become like each other only as we truly take upon ourselves the Savior's characteristics. If we are true to our basic natures, as the Lord has outlined them for us, our basic masculinity and femininity will not come into question. We should all possess both strength and sensitivity, courage and compassion, tenacity and tenderness. And as we best incorporate all those traits within our beings, we will be true to the male or female in us, which has been part of us since the beginning. If our sexual identity is based solely on our outward visible activities, our situation is serious indeed. The Savior was no more effeminate when he clasped the children to his bosom while in the Americas and blessed them and wept than was my great-great-grandmother unwomanly when she, as a widow, took the reins in her own hands and drove a team of oxen across the plains to Utah. If we feel that a woman lacks femininity because she is magnificent on the playing field or that a man lacks masculinity because he is a great artist, we are missing the point completely.

If the true male role is, indeed, to be obedient and sacrificial, how can a man achieve his highest potential with only macho traits? And if the woman is to reach her highest potential in her creative and nurturing role, how can she achieve it by being helpless and dependent?

President Kimball, in essence, has been urging women to get in condition, to get involved in the life around them, and to have a greater influence for good on what is happening in the world. He has urged women to become educated, to become gospel scholars, to develop every talent with which the Lord has blessed them and then to use their talents for the benefit of mankind. We need to learn and then teach each other the exalted role of women as revealed by the restored gospel of

Jesus Christ. We need to be sure our spouses understand it. And if we have children, we need to be sure that our sons and our daughters understand it.

The Prophet Joseph said in 1842 that the key was now turned in behalf of women and that knowledge and intelligence should flow down henceforth. President Kimball put it this way to the women of the Church in September 1979: "Much of the major growth that is coming to the Church in the last days will come because many of the good women of the world . . . will be drawn to the Church in large numbers. This will happen to the degree that the women of the Church reflect righteousness and articulateness in their lives and to the degree that the women of the Church are seen as distinct and different—in happy ways—from the women of the world." (*My Beloved Sisters,* p. 44.) In the same talk he said: "You must be wise in the choices you make, but we do not desire you to be uninformed or ineffective. You will be better mothers and wives, both in this life and in eternity, if you sharpen the skills you have been given and use the talents with which God has blessed you." (*My Beloved Sisters,* p. 43.)

We have been taught that where much is given, much is expected. If we as Latter-day Saints really understand the gospel of Jesus Christ and all that it portends for women, we will realize that no blessing can be withheld from us if we are prepared and worthy to receive it. The Lord expects us to be exemplars and teachers. I pray that we may catch the understanding and vision of who we really are—and so be.

Ida Smith is on the staff of Brigham Young University, most recently serving as director of continuing education for the BYU Alumni Association.

Drifting, Dreaming, Directing

ARDETH GREENE KAPP

f our day, Elder Bruce R. McConkie said, "Great trials lie ahead.
All of the sorrows and perils of
the past are but a foretaste of what
is yet to be. And we must prepare
ourselves temporally and spiritually."
(*Ensign,* May 1979, p. 92.) And even with
the reality of that kind of a backdrop, President Spencer W.
Kimball admonishes us, "Make no small plans, for they
hold no magic to stir men's souls." (Regional Representatives Seminar, 1979.) This reminds me of Dickens's *A Tale
of Two Cities.* The story begins with the contrasts of that
day:

"It was the best of times, it was the worst of times; it
was the age of wisdom, it was the age of foolishness; it was
the epic of belief, it was the epic of incredulity; it was the
season of light, it was the season of darkness; it was the
spring of hope, it was the winter of despair; we had everything before us, we had nothing before us; we were all
going direct to heaven, we were all going direct the other
way—in short—the period was so far like the present
period, that some of its noisiest authorities insisted on it
being received for good or for evil in a superlative degree
of comparison only. . . . It was the year of our Lord one
thousand seven hundred and seventy-five."

We are living in the times spoken of in the scriptures

when peace shall be taken from the earth. Of our time our prophet has said: "To be a righteous woman is a glorious thing in any age. To be a righteous woman during the winding-up scenes on this earth, before the second coming of our Savior, is an especially noble calling. The righteous woman's strength and influence today can be tenfold what it might be in more tranquil times." (Spencer W. Kimball, *My Beloved Sisters,* Deseret Book, 1979, p. 17.) Each of us will determine whether this day spoken of as the great and dreadful day will be recorded in our journal of life as a truly great and glorious day in which we are privileged to take part, or if, in fact, it is recorded only as a day of turmoil, conflict, and confusion.

President Harold B. Lee was referring to our day, I believe, when he said: "We have some tight places to go before the Lord is through with this church and the world in this dispensation, which is the last dispensation, which shall usher in the coming of the Lord. The gospel was restored to prepare a people ready to receive him. The power of Satan will increase; we see it in evidence on every hand. There will be inroads within the Church. There will be, as President Tanner has said, 'Hypocrites—those professing, but secretly are full of dead men's bones.' We will see those who profess membership, but secretly are plotting and trying to lead people not to follow the leadership that the Lord has set up to preside in this church."

Knowing the nature of man, the prophet continues, speaking as a seer: "You may not like what comes from the authority of the Church. It may contradict your political views. It may contradict your social views. It may interfere with some of your social life. But if you listen to these things, as if from the mouth of the Lord himself, with patience and faith, the promise is that 'the gates of hell shall not prevail against you; yea, and the Lord God will disperse the powers of darkness from before you, and cause the heavens to shake for your good, and his name's glory' (D&C 21:6)." ("Uphold the Hands of the President of the Church," *Improvement Era,* December 1970, p. 126.)

It is while a person stands undecided, uncommitted, and uncovenanted, with choices waiting to be made, that the vulnerability to every wind that blows becomes life-threatening.

Uncertainty, the thief of time and commitment, breeds vacilla-
tion and confusion. It is in taking a stand and making a choice to
follow our leaders that we become free to move forward. We
are then released from the crippling position of doubtful indecision and confusion. We then have access to power and
influence, so much so that we can hardly keep pace with our
opportunities. It is in or by using our agency and making firm
decisions that we turn the key.

Let me share with you a few lines from *The Agony and the
Ecstasy* by Irving Stone. On the very brink of creating what for
many has become his greatest masterpiece, Michelangelo is
faced with a decision that once made, must be lived with. He
had completed a multitude of drawings suggesting hundreds of
ways he might carve the *David*. He had been vacillating,
contemplating, considering all the alternatives, the many options, weighing and waiting. Now he must make a choice.

> He burned his earlier drawings, settled down to the
> simplest beginning, probing within himself. . . . What
> could he find in David triumphant, he asked himself,
> worthy of sculpturing. Tradition portrayed him after the
> fact. Yet David after the battle was an anticlimax, his great
> moment already gone. Which, then, was the important
> David? When did David become a giant? After killing
> Goliath, or at the moment he decided that he must try.
> David, as he was releasing with brilliant and deadly accu-
> racy the shot from the sling; or David before he entered
> the battle when he decided that the Israelites must be
> freed from their vassalage to the Philistines? Was not the
> decision more important than the act itself, since char-
> acter was more critical than action? For him, then, it was
> David's decision that made him a giant, not his killing of
> Goliath. This was the David he had been seeking, caught at
> the exultant height of resolution. . . . The man who killed
> Goliath would be committed all his life to warfare and its
> consequence: power. . . . To act was to join. David would
> not be sure he wanted to join. He had been a man alone.
> Once he tackled Goliath, there would be no turning
> back. . . . It was what he sensed that he would do to him-
> self, as well as what the world would do to him, that made
> him doubtful and averse in changing the pattern of his

days. His had been a hard choice indeed. (New York: Doubleday and Company, 1961, pp. 388, 390-91.)

It was in realizing the importance of David's hard choice and his faith to act that the door was unlocked, allowing Michelangelo to decide about his own mission in marble. Recognizing David as the giant at the moment of his decision allowed Michelangelo to make his decision; and the choice having been made, his tempo changed and with it came strength, power, and hidden energies:

> He soared, he drew with authority and power, he molded in clay...his fingers unable to keep pace with his thoughts and emotions, and with astonishing facility he knew where the David lay. The limitations of the block began to appear as assets, forcing his mind into a simplicity of design that might never have occurred to him had it been whole and perfect. The marble came alive now. (Ibid., p. 391.)

Each of us must release her own *David* from the imperfect marble that holds it captive, and each of us will greatly hasten that process as we follow the counsel of the prophet. President Kimball has said, "Be wise in the choices you make. . . . Sharpen the skills you have been given and use the talents with which God has blessed you." (*My Beloved Sisters,* Deseret Book, 1979, p. 43.) As we make right choices, we are driven by an exhilaration that causes us to hunger and thirst and feel new energies that lift us, like Michelangelo, toward our goal. "When his right hand tired of driving the hammer, he shifted it to the left, the chisel in his right moving with the same precision and probing sensitivity. He carved at night by candlelight." (*The Agony and the Ecstasy,* p. 394.)

I view this conference as an experience that has brought each of us in closer touch with the marble, though imperfect, with which we must work. It is in continuing to make right choices, decisions, and commitments that we are released to move forward at a hastened pace and lengthen our stride. If we remain motionless on the brink of indecision, we allow our voice, our example, our potential for good to be held imprisoned, as it were, in a slab of marble. Our testimonies, our commitments, and our covenants may lie deep inside, but until we can cut away all the debris that obscures this treasure, it cannot be recognized by others or even trusted by ourselves. On the consequences of a vacillating position, President J. Reuben Clark said: "The spiritual and psychological effect of a weak and vacillating testimony may well be actually harmful instead of helpful." (David H. Yarn, Jr., ed., *J. Reuben Clark: Selected Papers,* Brigham Young University Press, 1984, p. 250.)

Of this I am sure, and feel impressed to promise: as we seek divine direction, we will find our own block of marble to be more magnificent, with greater potential, than any of us have yet realized. The prophet has called each of us to be "known as women of God," and when the history of this era is reviewed, it might be said of us, as it was of Queen Esther, "Who knoweth whether thou art come to the kingdom for such a time as this?" (Esther 4:14.)

Even with these truths and inspiring examples before us, I feel concern for some who may feel discouraged and that we get our moralities mixed up with our realities, that the gulf between morality and reality is too big, the stakes too high, the requirements too rigid, and the rewards too uncertain. In response to this earnest concern, I have prepared some thoughts that might be considered as we each examine and reexamine our own choices and decisions and opinions. In an attempt to give order to these ponderings, I have labeled them "Drifting, Dreaming, and Directing."

It has been my observation, and it is my confession as a former participant, that many people drift along with the crowd in the Church. Many good people drift to sacrament meeting and Sunday School, even family home evening, and they drift through a casual study of the scriptures. The drifters fall into at least one of two groups. In the first are those who step into the mainstream, getting deeply involved with Church activity and floating with the current, comfortable with a sense of false security that they are in the right place. Others, who form the second group, accepting a few selected principles, resist being part of the flow, the mainstream, and choose to get out into the eddies at the edge, freed from the demands of full participation. It is difficult to decide which of these two groups is better—or worse. Those of us who are, on the basis of activity alone, very much in the Church may not necessarily have the Church very much in us; and if we left, the Church might hardly recognize the difference. Following the practices, doing the right thing but without coming to know, understand, accept, and apply the saving principles and doctrines, we may be compared to one who spends his entire life stringing the instrument—never once hearing the music for which the instrument was created or incapable of recognizing it if he did.

In matters of principle, let us stand as solid as a rock. In matters of practice, may all that we do be based upon these saving principles, and may we understand the intrinsic relationship of principles and practices. It is in making the decision to follow the admonition of the prophet and to become scholars of the scriptures that we gradually learn the doctrine that prepares us to stand on the rock of revelation and to experience less and less the restless sense of drifting, wandering, questioning, and searching.

Many good people are very faithful in following the traditions and practices. I'm reminded of a song we used to sing in Sunday School: "Never be late for the Sunday School class/ Come with your bright smiling faces." The chorus ended with: "Try to be there, always be there/Promptly at ten in the morning." Ten in the morning became a practice, a tradition, for a long time. It was not a principle. Yet there were those among the faithful who felt uncomfortable about change, not unlike the feelings expressed by some today as practices and traditions are modified. When changes come, and they always will, for some it may be a test to survive because their foundation is based on practices alone, without an understanding of the eternal, unchanging principles.

Being faithful does not necessarily develop faith. The first principle of the gospel is faith in the Lord, Jesus Christ. To have faith in him is to know him, to know his doctrine, and to know that the course of our life is in harmony with and acceptable to him. It is relatively easy to be faithful, but faith is born out of study, fasting, prayer, meditation, sacrifice, service, and, finally, personal revelation. Glimpses of understanding come line upon line, precept upon precept. Our Father is anxious to feed us just as fast as we can handle it, but we regulate the richness and the volume of our spiritual diet. And we do this by the same method used by the sons of Mosiah: "They had waxed strong in the knowledge of the truth; . . . they had searched the scriptures diligently, that they might know the word of God. But this is not all; they had given themselves to much prayer, and fasting; therefore they had the spirit of prophecy, and the spirit of revelation, and when they taught, they taught with power and authority of God." (Alma 17:2-3.)

Faithfulness without faith, practices without principles, will leave us and our families seriously wanting as we move closer to that time spoken of by Heber C. Kimball when he said, "The time is coming when no man or woman will be able to endure on borrowed light. Each will have to be guided by the light within himself. If you do not have it, you will not stand." (Quoted by Harold B. Lee, *Conference Report,* October 1955, p. 56.)

May we find ourselves doing less and less drifting as we make right choices based on personal revelation that give direction to us and our families each day of our lives. And with that direction, let us develop "a program for personal improvement" that will cause us to "reach for new levels of achievement," as the prophet has admonished us. (Spencer W. Kimball, *My Beloved Sisters,* p. 20.) He has also promised us that the Lord "will help us as we decide from day to day on the allocation of our time and talent.We will move faster if we hurry less. We will make more real progress if we focus on the fundamentals." (*Ensign,* May 1979, p. 83.) Certain principles are essential in our struggle to avoid the wasteful experience of drifting.

Now what of dreamers? Many of us are dreamers at times, wanting in some way to escape ourselves, to be free of our own limitations. I often ponder the words: "With voluntary dreams they cheat their minds." It has been said that if fate would destroy a man, it would first separate his forces and drive him to think one way and act another. It would rob him of the contentment that comes only from unity within. Choices must be decisive so that dreams and actions can be in harmony with each other. When we do something different than we know we should, it is like going into a final examination and putting down the wrong answer, even though we know the right one.

Dreaming, however, can also serve a very positive function when it fits Webster's definition of having "a goal or purpose ardently desired."

In the popular musical *South Pacific* is the delightful little song that goes, "If you don't have a dream, how ya gonna make a dream come true?" I am concerned for some of our sisters who have a magnificent dream but who will never fully realize its fulfillment because they feel that their righteous husband will take care of it, and they fail to prepare for their part in this eternal partnership.

There are some sisters who ponder the administrative structure of the Church and trouble themselves with what they think they don't have without ever coming to a full understanding of their own special and unique mission and the great blessings reserved specifically for them. We hear it expressed in terms that suggest that because women don't have the priesthood, they are shortchanged.

There are still others of our sisters who have the misunderstanding that priesthood is synonymous with men, and so they excuse themselves and have no concern for studying its importance in their own lives. The term *priesthood* is used without qualification, whether it refers to a bearer of the priesthood, priesthood blessings, or priesthood ordinances. Our hearts should cry out in either case, and we should raise our voices and shout warnings to sisters whose dreams are built on such faulty foundations.

Our greatest dreams will be fulfilled only as we come to understand fully and experience the blessings of the priesthood, the power of the priesthood, and the ordinances of the priesthood in our own lives. If we were to begin with the time a child is given a name and a blessing and then continue on through baptism, confirmation, the sacrament, callings and being set apart, patriarchal blessings, administrations, the endowment, and finally celestial marriage, we would quickly realize that all of the saving blessings of the priesthood are for boys and girls, men and women. And while that divine mission of motherhood is paramount, it is not all-inclusive. To help another gain eternal life is a companion privilege. This privilege, indeed this sacred responsibility, this noblest of callings, is denied to no worthy person. To assist in bringing to pass the eternal life of man, and to do it in dignity and honor, is the very pinnacle of my own personal dream. And for us to close our eyes to these eternal truths and not recognize them as priesthood blessings and ordinances is to keep us on the fringe area of the very saving principles—the only principles—that can make our eternal dreams come true.

It is true that as sisters we do not experience a priesthood ordination that carries an administrative function, nor do we have the tremendous, weighty burden of having that sacred responsibility heaped upon us in addition to the mission of creating and nurturing in partnership with God, first in giving birth to the Lord's spirit children and then in raising those children to serve the Lord and keep his commandments.

I have come to know that we can all, both men and women, rejoice in the sacred calling of motherhood. To give birth is but one part of this sacred calling.

After drifting and dreaming, now may we consider the directing of one's life. At my high school graduation, Oscar A. Kirkham stood at the pulpit, looking into the eyes of idealistic, enthusiastic graduates, and in his husky voice he offered this challenge: "Build a seaworthy ship. Be a loyal shipmate, and sail a true course." I don't remember anything else that he said, or what anyone else said, for that matter. But I've pondered that challenge many times over the years. In directing our lives, we want to be sure of the true course and its ultimate destination. We cannot risk being caught in the disillusionment of the fellow who was committed to going north and was in fact traveling north—but on an iceberg that was floating south.

"True points," like stars in the heavens to guide us, are readily available for anyone earnestly seeking direction. These true points of doctrine are found in the true church. (See D&C 11:16.) Conversion to the truth comes by accepting true doctrine, and the truth of doctrine can be known only by revelation gained as a result of obedience. The Savior taught: "My doctrine is not mine, but his that sent me. If any man will do his will, he shall know of the doctrine, whether it be of God, or whether I speak of myself." (John 7:16-17.)

The skeptic of two thousand years ago might have said, "Look, if I knew for sure that the star (the sign of the Savior's birth) would appear in the heavens tonight, I would be obedient." That's like standing in front of a stove and saying, "Give me some heat, and then I'll put in the wood." We must put in the wood first, and then we feel the warmth and the heat; then we can bear testimony of its reality. In Ether we read: "Dispute not because ye see not, for ye receive no witness until after the trial of your faith." (Ether 12:6.) As our faith is tried and we are found standing firm even in times of storm, we will rejoice with increased confidence and discover within ourselves the loyal shipmate that we really have as we sail a true course.

Apostles and prophets have been provided in the Church for the purpose of identifying and teaching true doctrine, lest men be "tossed to and fro, and carried about with every wind of doctrine." (Ephesians 4:14.) Now, we can follow the Brethren blindly, as one of my non-Mormon friends claims that we do— and I might add that it is far safer and better to follow them blindly than not at all—but that could be an abdication of our responsibility to direct our own lives and become spiritually independent. Again, following the practices alone is not enough. We must come to know the reason, indeed the doctrinal basis, for that practice; otherwise, when the practice or tradition is questioned or changed, those who do not understand the principle are prone to waver. They may even abandon or reject the very practice intended as a schoolmaster to carry them to an understanding of a saving and eternal principle.

There were those in King Benjamin's time who were caught up in exacting the law of Moses. With blinders they followed the practices—an eye for an eye and a tooth for a tooth—until King Benjamin taught them that their practices availed them nothing unless they accepted the mission of the Savior and his atonement. Without that commitment, their practices were for naught.

While Adam was offering the firstlings of the flock, an angel appeared and asked him why he was doing it, why this practice. You will remember Adam's response. He said, "I know not, save the Lord commanded me." The practice was offering sacrifice, but the principle, in this instance, was obedience. And then Adam received a witness, after the trial of his faith. The angel explained: "This thing is a similitude of the sacrifice of the Only Begotten of the Father." (Moses 5:6-7.)

As we direct our lives, it is important to understand practices and principles, their relationship as well as the differences between them. In my mind's eye, I visualize the practices as a horizontal line, a foundation, a schooling, a testing, a preparation; and the saving and exalting eternal principles or doctrine as a vertical line that links our souls to heaven and builds the relationship with God and faith in the Lord, Jesus Christ, and his mission.

There will continue to be much opposition to true doctrine; but by and by the storm subsides, the clouds disperse, the sun breaks forth, and the rock of truth is seen again, firm and lasting. There never was a true principle that was not met by storm after storm of opposition and abuse, until that principle had obtained such influence that it no longer paid to oppose it. But until that time, the opposition and the abuse have ebbed and flowed like the tide. It was a strong doctrine that rid Jesus of his weak disciples, and the same testing process continues today in determining those worthy of his kingdom.

The Prophet Joseph Smith stated: "God has in reserve a time . . . when He will bring all His subjects, who have obeyed His voice and kept His commandments, into His celestial rest. This rest is of such perfection and glory, that man has need of a preparation before he can, according to the laws of that kingdom, enter it and enjoy its blessings. This being the fact, God has given certain laws to the human family, which, if observed are sufficient to prepare them to inherit this rest. This, then, we conclude, was the purpose of God in giving His laws to us."

(*Teachings of the Prophet Joseph Smith,* Deseret Book, 1976, p. 54.)

In our goal to apply principles and proceed with direction, it isn't intended that we arrive before we experience that witness of the Spirit. The witness sustains us in our journey. In a few lines of prose, given so eloquently, President Kimball tells how the gospel came into the life of an unlearned Bolivian woman. In hearing of the mission of the Savior and the doctrine of the Atonement, the Spirit bore witness to her soul. With her golden-brown face turned upward, her dark eyes wide and trusting, with tears rising to overflowing, she whispered her emotions: "You mean, he did that for me?" With the confirmation of her question received, she again whispered, this time not in question but in reverent awe, "You mean, he did that for me!"

To this eternal and saving principle, I bear my fervent testimony that he did that for you and for me. With that conviction, I think with soberness of the penetrating observation by Truman Madsen: "The greatest tragedy of life is that having paid that awful price of suffering 'according to the flesh that his bowels might be filled with compassion' and now prepared to reach down and help us, he is forbidden because we won't let him. We look down instead of up." ("Prayer and the Prophet Joseph," *Ensign,* January 1976, p. 23.) We choose to remain enclosed in marble. But if we would free ourselves and come to know this truth through personal revelation, the time might come when even our routine practices could become life-giving and done in the Lord's name with his spirit so that the whole of our lives becomes a sacred experience as we labor for him continuously.

Not long ago I witnessed what until then had been something of a routine for me, the blessing on the food. Picture with me my aged father, his body deteriorated by the devastation of stomach cancer, while his spirit was magnified and refined through suffering. He sat at the kitchen table; he then weighed less than a hundred pounds. Bowing his head, resting it in his frail, trembling hands over a spoonful of baby food—all that he could eat—he pronounced a blessing on the food, as though it were a sacred sacrament, and gave thanks with acceptance and submission, with truth and faith, because he knew to whom he was speaking.

It is in coming to know our Savior and the saving principles that he taught through the gospel of Jesus Christ that we become different. And we need to be recognized as being different. The majority of the world doesn't see the options. It is our responsibility to be obviously good and obviously right—and able to articulate our values and be advocates for truth. We may have a temple recommend and attend our meetings and practice the principles, but how we look and act, what we say and do, may be the only message some people will receive. Our acts should show that there is a power and an influence with us that the inhabitants of the world do not understand. What is it that distinguishes us from others? The distinction is that we profess to be guided by revelation. It is because of this principle that we are peculiar, since all of our actions can be under divine guidance. Having made the choice, we must stand and be visibly different. Until we make that choice, we remain anonymous, subject to the current of the meandering multitudes.

President Kimball has said: "Much of the major growth that is coming to the Church in the last days will come because many of the good women of the world (in whom there is often such an inner sense of spirituality) will be drawn to the Church in large numbers. This will happen to the degree that the women of the Church reflect righteousness and articulateness in their lives and to the degree that they are seen as distinct and different—in happy ways—from the women of the world." (*My Beloved Sisters,* p. 44.) That is our direction. That is our challenge.

All individuals are what they are and where they are by a composite of choices that direct their lives each day. The responsibility of directing is not only for our own lives, but also for others who may be looking for the light. As we build a seaworthy ship and then sail a true course, many sails will navigate safely through troubled waters into the peaceful harbor because of the unflickering light radiating from the bow of our craft. As I consider our responsibility to others, I am inspired by the words of the song:

> Brightly beams our Father's mercy
> From his lighthouse evermore,
> But to us he gives the keeping
> Of the lights along the shore.
>
> Let the lower lights be burning;
> Send a gleam across the wave.
> Some poor fainting, struggling seaman
> You may rescue, you may save.
>
> Dark the night of sin has settled;
> Loud the angry billows roar.
> Eager eyes are watching, longing,
> For the lights along the shore.
>
> Trim your feeble lamp, my brother;
> Some poor sailor, tempest tossed,
> Trying now to make the harbor,
> In the darkness may be lost.
> (*Hymns*, 1985, no. 335.)

Elder Neal A. Maxwell has written, "As other lights flicker and fade, the light of the gospel will burn ever more brightly in a darkening world, guiding the humble but irritating the guilty and those who prefer the dusk of decadence." (*Church News*, January 5, 1970, p. 28.)

May our lights be bright without a flicker, as we tend the lights along the shore. Let us each one reach out and touch another. Let us help carry one another's burdens. In cooperation we can overcome great odds. Let us rejoice with one another. It may be just a smile, a note, a call, an encouraging word that says, "I care; I understand; I will stand by you and help you." These are life-saving measures in times of storms.

Recently I was privileged to read part of a blessing received by one of our sisters that stated that her life would continue over a period when she would see great devastation and that she would be called to go into homes of the sorrowing, the suffering, the sick and afflicted, to minister unto them, to bind up their wounds, and to cheer them. I believe that we have all been called to minister unto those in need, to bind up not just their physical wounds but also their spiritual wounds, social wounds, and wounds that are kept hidden, sometimes festering until someone cares enough to tend the lights along the shore.

These are matters of eternal consequence, and we can, if we desire, reach far enough to experience an awakening of things we have known before. Remember, President Kimball said: "In the world before we came here, faithful women were given certain assignments while faithful men were foreordained to certain priesthood tasks. While we do not remember the particulars, this does not alter the glorious reality of what we once agreed to. We are accountable for those things which long ago were expected of us just as are those whom we sustain as prophets and apostles." (*My Beloved Sisters,* p. 37.)

It is my fervent and humble testimony that the heavens are very much open to women today. They are not closed unless we ourselves, by our choices, close them. And this reality can be just as evident as in any time past. As I read of the great spirituality of women of the past and realize how the Lord communicated with them, I thrill with the spiritual manifestations that have accompanied their missions in life, literally a power evidencing the will of God made known through their instrumentality. I think of Eliza R. Snow, of whom Joseph F. Smith said, "She walked not in the borrowed light of others, but faced the morning unafraid and invincible."

The Spirit whispers to me that there are Eliza R. Snows among us even today, and there can be many, many more. We can pull down the blessings of heaven through obedience to law. These divine and sacred blessings are not reserved for others alone. Visions and revelations come by the power of the Holy Ghost. The Lord has said, "On my servants and on my hand-maidens I will pour out in those days of my Spirit; and they shall prophesy." (Acts 2:18.)

Let us go forth with the faith, the vision, the direction, and the decision to abide the laws that ensure these blessings not only for ourselves and our families but for all of God's children everywhere. Let us each feel deeply the power and strength and influence for good of our collective and united resolves. With renewed determination and confidence and commitment to the covenants we have made, let us become truly and in every way "women of God." Let us go forth in faith and confidence and prepare for the noble calling spoken of by the Prophet—to be righteous women during the winding-up scenes on this earth before the second coming of our Savior.

Ardeth Greene Kapp has a master's degree in curriculum development from Brigham Young University, and has been a popular teacher, writer, and speaker. In April 1984 she was called to serve as general president of the Young Women.

Daughters of God

ELAINE A. CANNON

At a world's fair, treasured art was featured in two pavilions sponsored by religious organizations. One exhibit included Michelangelo's haunting *Piéta*—Christ crucified, lying across the lap of grief-stricken Mary. The Mormon exhibit featured Thorvaldsen's incredibly compelling *Christus*—the risen Lord with his arms outstretched, showing his nail-pierced hands to the multitudes who would come unto him. I learned a powerful lesson about attitude when I overheard a guide explain to a tour group, "This religious group has the dead Christ, and the Mormons have the risen Savior."

One looks at the works of artists through the centuries who have dealt with the nativity—Mary, Joseph, and the baby Jesus. How different they appear when seen through a variety of artists' eyes. The artists deal with the same people and the same tender theme, but their interpretations vary from ornately robed and haloed figures to simply sketched suggestions of the Holy Happening.

We look at ourselves—Mormon women all bound together by church affiliation and similar standards—yet how different we are!

Day by day I deal with these differences in women in the way they see things and what this does to their lives as they struggle to work out personal salvation according to their own views of prophets, principles, and problems.

Oh, how we differ! Our roots and the sum of our memories mark us. Sometimes the anguish of the struggle is more painful than pain itself. Sometimes, for a while, confusion rules. Sometimes people are only *convinced* the gospel is true. They are not yet converted.

As I look at you, I see such a cross section. This makes our sociality here interesting as well as challenging. It is recorded in the Doctrine and Covenants: "That same sociality which exists among us here will exist among us there, only it will be coupled with eternal glory, which glory we do not now enjoy." (D&C 130:2.) Since this is so, should we not now love each other more and not be angry or judgmental over differences? I sense some anger.

The things that matter most must not be sacrificed for those that matter least. It seems to me that it is time, then, for the women of the Church to behave with a sense of belonging instead of a sense of separateness. We are not women of the world, after all. We are sisters. We are daughters of God. We are children of the covenant who are marching to the same drummer, though we may be singing a separate song. Matthew Arnold wrote this truth: "Such a price the Gods exact for song: To become what we sing."

As we spend this time together, may we find something that will help us as we sing our songs and live our lives, help us in our similarities as well as in our differentness, in our public and private problems, and in our copings and our contributions.

May the Spirit of the Lord, whom I love and bear witness of, fill us with love, with joy, and with understanding so that we may feel close to each other and be moved to become more like him.

Sisters, one powerful alikeness we share is the inimitable hope and promise we enjoy through affiliation with this, his church on earth. I am sure you agree. It is like the world's fair: whether we see things as Michelangelo or as Thorvaldsen, we are concerned with Christ. How we look at life will be affected by how we consider Christ.

And so I am going to talk with you about baptism today— about baptism and confirmation and the laying on of hands for the gift of the Holy Ghost, and of covenants, commitments, the sacrament, disciplines, freedoms, light, and love. I'm going to talk about taking upon us the name of Jesus Christ and what that means to us as women in The Church of Jesus Christ of Latter-day Saints.

1. *The Ordinance of Baptism*

Being a member of The Church of Jesus Christ of Latter-day Saints, baptized by immersion, took on a new importance to me a few years ago. Before the Washington Temple was closed to the public and dedicated for its service, I wandered through on tour.

The day was gorgeous, colors were rampant in the surrounding woods, and the building was breathtaking with pristine spires rising to the sky. And the spirit there was surging. I was excited and grateful to be there. Everyone else was curious. Washington, D.C., is home for people from all over the world who staff the embassies based there, and hundreds of people with wide-ranging national backgrounds came, some in family groups. There were service people of high rank with their aides dusting the paths ahead, and professional people in the arts hiding behind dark glasses. Each looked different, but all reacted similarly. They were thoughtful. They were touched. There were searching questions in discussions with missionaries after. They took every brochure they were offered. They bought copies of the Book of Mormon eagerly. They wanted to buy replicas of what they called the angel "Gabriel." (They hadn't heard of Moroni.) There were none for sale, of course.

One handsome young Scandinavian ski pro with sun-streaked hair and a hand-knit turtleneck sweater stood next to us as we silently toured the last section of the building. The final room housed the white baptismal font resting on twelve oxen. He looked hurriedly about as we went into the room and asked, "Where can I find out more about this church?" Swiftly to his side came several who knew just how to tell him more.

A distinguished-looking gentleman standing by me before the baptismal font said, "I feel I am being guided or swept into something beyond my control—something very deep and wonderful. I've never had a feeling like this. What do I have to do to get in there?" He pointed toward the twelve oxen silently supporting the font.

"Die," I replied.

The Mormons nearby laughed, of course, while I quickly went on to tell him about baptism for the dead and for the living. We talked about repentance and faith, about how Christ died for us and came forth so that we might not have to suffer the spiritual death that our serious mistakes—our sins— impose. We talked about not feeling clean enough to meet the Savior if that were suddenly to happen tomorrow. He shook his head sadly. "I'm not good enough," he said. "If I could just start over. I just don't feel clean enough inside."

I explained the symbolism of the ordinance of baptism—of being buried in the water and coming forth a new being, of being washed clean in the process. Being a man whose business is with people and the symbols used to motivate them, he understood at once and said, "Sprinkling just doesn't do it, does it."

Then we took him to talk with the missionaries.

Sprinkling may not do it, but neither does perfunctory performance or casual acceptance of the vital ordinance of baptism.

Every woman of whatever age, including the precious little sisters eight and over, should thoroughly understand the sacred act of baptism. Mothers, grandmothers, aunts, babysitters, and special friends of children can teach the blessing of baptism better if they understand it. To our nonmember friends we can be eternally helpful if we can properly explain the purpose and symbolism of baptism and testify of him whose name we take upon us when the ordinance is performed.

We talk of these things because they are the very basis of our lives, the basis of Christ's doctrine for us. In a climate where some barter their church membership for political expediency or for a moment's pleasure in sin, or who forfeit church-related blessings because they do not fully understand yet, it is well for us to review these things again lest we too fall. Understanding brings more appropriate behavior. We will be more valiant. We will give more willingly and serve more compassionately and effectively. We will love better.

2. *Taking Upon Us His Name*

In the first few chapters of Mosiah in the Book of Mormon, the powerful sermon of King Benjamin is recorded. Those ancient Americans were deeply moved as they listened to King Benjamin teach of Christ, who was yet to be born. And they cried out in one voice that they wanted to make a covenant with Christ and take upon themselves his name. Then King Benjamin said:

"Ye have spoken the words that I desired; and the covenant which ye have made is a righteous covenant. And now, because of the covenant which ye have made ye shall be called the children of Christ, his sons, and his daughters. . . . There is no other name given whereby salvation cometh; therefore, I would that ye should take upon you the name of Christ, all you that have entered into the covenant with God that ye should be obedient unto the end of your lives. And it shall come to pass that whosoever doeth this shall be found at the right hand of God, for he shall know the name by which he is called; for he shall be called by the name of Christ." (Mosiah 5:6-9.)

When the Savior first came to the Nephite people, he spoke of baptism and its covenant act more than a dozen times in one chapter, as recorded in Third Nephi, chapter 11. He said: "Whoso believeth in me, and is baptized, the same shall be saved; and they are they who shall inherit the kingdom of God. . . . This is my doctrine, . . . and whoso believeth in me believeth in the Father also, and unto him will the Father bear record of me, for he will visit him with fire and with the Holy Ghost." (3 Nephi 11:33-35.)

We came to earth trailing clouds of glory. We go, one day, to whatever eternal reward is ours. Our Creator has given us the principles and procedures to get through life and to guide us back into his presence. His church is the institution, the framework with which the fulness of his guiding gospel may be found and the necessary ordinances performed with valid authority that binds them in heaven as well as on earth.

His church is named after him—The Church of Jesus Christ

of Latter-day Saints. We meet in the name of the Lord. We pray in his name. We covenant in his name. We take his name upon us in sacred ordinances. As sisters, what does this mean to us specifically? What difference does this make in our lives? How does this set us apart from other women in the world—this taking upon us the name of Jesus Christ?

Traveling for the Church has given me a perspective that has set me thinking about names. We meet delightful women and girls named Tammie, Maren, Carolyn, Susan, Chieko, Lani, Birgitta, Marja, Cheri, Anja. And we have met a whole new batch of little ones named Camilla—proof that the visits President and Sister Kimball have made are remembered with warmth and purpose. There are many little boys named Spencer these days too, all over the Church.

Some time ago, we had a party at our home for a special family occasion. We were honored that President and Sister Kimball came. As I was welcoming them, my sister quickly brought her little son over to meet them. "President Kimball," she said, "this is Mark Spencer Cook."

President Kimball bent his knees so that he could look eye-to-eye with this little boy. Then he took the child's hand firmly in his own and said, "Well, Mark Spencer Cook, do you know what I give to little boys named Spencer?"

"No," came a shy reply.

"I give them a dollar. Camilla, do you have a dollar?"

Obviously Sister Kimball is very important to her husband. When she took upon herself his name, Mrs. Spencer Woolley Kimball, she accepted all the delights as well as the vital duties that a wife is entitled to.

Now, though a little girl be named Camilla and a boy be called Spencer, this does not guarantee she or he will be like them—partner to a prophet or prophet of the Lord. But there is, of course, much that can be said for the power of suggestion. This is true as well for those of us who have formally taken upon us the name of Jesus Christ.

3. *Gifts of the Holy Ghost*

As we take upon us his name, we share in it. In return, he

endows us with the gifts of the Holy Ghost—with the power to testify of him to others, power to be effective in our service and callings, power to discern needs of our loved ones, power to discern truth from error. And we receive promptings necessary for making sound value judgments in the many facets of our lives. We need only to listen to the still, small voice and cultivate this spirit within us. Surely we daughters of our Heavenly Father, whether we are young or old, needful or momentarily fulfilled, can better meet the mighty work of womanhood if we have his spirit with us.

I had a tender experience as a young mother that I think proves this point. I had a new baby brought to me for nursing for the first time since the delivery. As I began the motherly task of feeding the baby, I was prompted by the Spirit that this baby was not mine. I love all babies, but if I have a choice, I'd prefer to care closely for my own. I checked the identification tag, the wrist bracelet, and the name tape on the baby's back. All indicated I had the right infant, but the Spirit told me otherwise. Subsequent hospital investigation of the baby's footprints confirmed that a mistake had been made. The Spirit working through a mother righted a terrible wrong.

Now, if we take upon us the name of Jesus Christ, we take upon us the obligation of being obedient to his will for us, to his timetable for the fulfillment of our dreams, to the way he answers our prayers.

When we covenant with the Lord to take upon us his name, we also take upon us the burden of helping mankind in our special, womanly way. Oh, sisters, can't we do better to bring ourselves together in heart and purpose though our activities may vary somewhat? Can we not go forth determined to help each other draw closer to Christ, as well as endure the daily grind?

It becomes increasingly clear that the work of women in the plan of life is as critically important as is the administrative and ordinance work of the priesthood. We love, we comfort, we create, we nurture, we teach, we right wrongs, and we provide the atmosphere for heaven on earth. The responsibility of birth falls to us. But the bountiful blessings of being born *again* come only through Melchizedek Priesthood ordinances. What a magnificent method for both women and men.

As we grow in understanding of our relationship with Christ, it makes all the difference in how we feel about our selves, how we behave, how we assess the antics of the spiritually starved, and how we embrace the principles God has given us to live by. Gradually, as we grow, and through his grace, we become more and more like him. This is a mighty work. It is his work.

I am not only comforted, but I am also excited at what I am seeing among the young women and the older sisters across this worldwide church. Though some are disgruntled, there seems to be a new upsurge of wonderful, committed women. Sisters, the wash *is* being done. The babies *are* being loved and trained. Young women *are* standing firm against peer pressure. People *are* sensitively spreading the good word. Prayers *are* being offered more carefully and testimonies expressed more fervently. We have in the Church today women of all ages who are aware, who care. They understand what it means to take upon them the name of Christ. Their lamps are filled. They are ready. They await the bridegroom.

4. *Making a Difference*

Meanwhile, they are making the difference in the quality of life of those about them. For example, I met a superb missionary who was older than the other elders. I learned that he had had a very troubled past. When I asked how the change came in him, he replied with tears in his eyes, "My mother prayed me straight. Endlessly, tirelessly, she prayed for me." His record of baptisms adds jewels to his mother's crown.

A family with three teenage children had dropped into inactivity in a Scandinavian stake. The home teachers, the visiting teachers, the priesthood leadership had not been able to reach these people. Then a young woman was called to be a class president. Her attitude was, "If I am called to serve, I will serve with success through the power of God." And she was successful. She reached that family; one of them now serves as branch leader for the young women.

A single woman joined the Church under difficult circumstances some years ago. When I talked with her recently, she told me of thirty-one members of her family and of nearly thirty others she had helped into the Church. "I told the Lord that if I came into the Church, I didn't want to be in alone. I've talked more to him than anyone else in these past years. I tell him that if he'll open the doors, I'll walk through and get the people."

As wonderful as these and other women like them are, we can all be even better. We need more women who, having been willing to take upon them the name of Jesus Christ, are then willing to take upon them the work he has designated for the sisters.

We need more women who know Jesus Christ and who will teach and testify of him. We need women who are studying the scriptures, who know the word of God and experiment upon the word; women who will move by knowledge and also by faith, who will "be no more as children, tossed to and fro, and carried about with every wind of doctrine, by the sleight of men, and cunning craftiness, whereby they lie in wait to deceive." (Ephesians 4:14.)

Dr. Charles D. McIver, in an address at the North Carolina College for Women, said, "When you educate a man, you educate an individual; when you educate a woman, you educate a whole family." Brigham Young admitted that if he had to educate either his sons or his daughters, he would choose his daughters because they would influence generations.

In the process of becoming educated, let us grow spiritually in our knowledge of Christ. This is the all-important knowledge. With this knowledge comes change.

We need women who are more valiant and who are not ashamed of the gospel of Jesus Christ, who can stand up and be counted, who use the spirit within them to discern. These are the peaceful women. Frustration and depression are not part of their being.

We need women who are willing to make a wholesome difference. Robert Frost's often-quoted poem regarding two roads comes to mind. The one *not* taken made all the difference. And isn't this true with Mormon women and the path we choose to take? Someone once suggested that for evil to flourish, it simply requires that good men and women do nothing. For good Mormon women to do nothing—to simply bask in their latter-day blessings—seems to me to be a pitiful breach of promise and purpose.

We need more diligent women to love their husbands into gentility or to just love their husbands and children better. If they haven't done either yet, then we need them to open their hearts and extend the reach of their affection and effectiveness to others.

So whether we are named Maren, Margit, Susan, Helen, Brigitta, or even Camilla, the Lord needs women who will take upon themselves his ways, his will, and his work, as well as his name.

If each of us will begin to do this with the power that is in us, we will soon notice a mighty change in our lives. Trials and troubles won't get the better of us. The gates of hell will not prevail against us, and the heaven will shake for our good. (See D&C 21:6.) Our hearts and our homes will be filled with unspeakable love. Our wards will be stronger and our numbers will swell. Good will be done.

You see, taking upon us the name of Christ, and then *living* as if we have, *can* make all the difference.

Elaine Cannon served as president of the Young Women of the Church from 1978 to 1984. She previously served with the Youth Correlation Committee, the YWMIA general board, the LDS Student Association, and the Church's General Activities Committee. She has been the author or co-author of several books, associate editor of the New Era, *and a newspaper columnist.*

Priesthood and Sisterhood:
An Equal Partnership

GRETHE BALLIF PETERSON

he year 1979 was a year of contrasts for Latter-day Saint women. Through missionary efforts in Ghana and Nigeria, we were introduced to black African women who were members of the Church. The photographs of handsome black women wrapped in batik turbans and gowns, worshipping in Relief Society, expanded our sense of sisterhood.

At about the same time, the excommunication of Sonia Johnson was acted out on the nightly news and discussed at length in the nation's newspapers. This was a painful process for Latter-day Saint women to witness. For many women it generated a need to sort out issues of identity and commitment with other women of the faith. Not only was there a need to be better understood, but there was also a need to share with other LDS women what it means to be spiritually committed. I have sensed a need for closer association with other women, a kind of bonding that is positive and strengthening.

At the same time, President Kimball spoke more precisely and extensively than ever before to the women of the Church. He described the great possibilities of womanhood and methodically discussed what women need to know and need to do. In the Church's women's conference in the fall of 1979, he stated unequivocally that men and women have full equality as spirit children. Then, quoting Elder John A. Widtsoe, he said, "The place of woman is to walk beside the man, not in front of him nor behind him." President Kimball continued: "Within those great assurances, however, our roles and assignments differ. These are eternal differences, with women being given many tremendous responsibilities of motherhood and sisterhood and the men the tremendous responsibilities of fatherhood and the priesthood." (*My Beloved Sisters,* Deseret Book, 1979, pp. 35, 37.)

President Kimball seemed to be making a distinction that I had not heard before. He was talking about the responsibilities of men and women, equating motherhood with fatherhood, which we certainly understand, and then sisterhood with priesthood. He seemed to be talking about a parallel relationship in the function of priesthood and sisterhood, a relationship that is obviously important, but one that we haven't thought much about.

Thinking more about President Kimball's words regarding sisterhood and priesthood, as well as the other possibilities he outlined for women, it becomes increasingly clear that the work of the Church and the gospel of Jesus Christ cannot go forth without understanding that men and women have an equal partnership within priesthood. Whether it is with husbands or bishops or brothers in the gospel, on every level of activity where the administration of priesthood ordinances is not necessary, men and women should be working together. The Church needs the male and female perspective, which I believe to be different in important and positive ways.

I suggest that President Kimball was saying something new and important about the association of women in the Church, something significant about sisterhood. Placing sisterhood in a parallel position with priesthood makes it a matter of primary importance. As men and women in the gospel, we need to know what it is and how it applies to our lives.

Priesthood is a subject that has been explored in depth. It is central to our doctrine, the sacred link between man and God. It provides us with the divine authority to act in the name of Jesus Christ. Without it, we could not do the work of the

Church. For purposes of this discussion, when I speak of priesthood, I am not talking about ecclesiastical priesthood, that is, the priesthood responsibilities of ordinances and church governances. I am talking about the personal application of priesthood as it works in the lives of individuals. It is priesthood that, when fully understood and lived, facilitates a Christ-centered life. It is an extension of "Godly influence" in all that one does.

The Lord made very clear the conditions of priesthood trust. In the Doctrine and Covenants we find the warning, "Behold, there are many called, but few are chosen. And why are they not chosen? Because their hearts are set so much upon the things of this world, and aspire to the honors of men." Then we are told that "only by persuasion, by long-suffering, by gentleness and meekness, and by love unfeigned, by kindness, and pure knowledge" can priesthood have any power and influence. The priesthood bearer is warned that if he exercises any unrighteous dominion (any degree of unrighteousness), the heavens will withdraw themselves, and it is, "Amen to the priesthood or the authority of that man." (See D&C 121:34-42.) The Lord has made clear what he expects and what the rules are.

Sisterhood presents a different challenge. Perhaps since the association of women has always been informal, without an ecclesiastical base, little is written about it. As suggested by Gerta Lerner, a professor of history at Sarah Lawrence College, talking about our needs as women to understand and know our own history since the beginning, "The heaviest burden of the loss of women's past, of the absence of the knowledge about the true role of women in building society, has fallen upon women. For most women, growing up has meant having too few role models. Women of this generation have been deprived of the reassurance and strength that comes from knowing about one's heritage."

It seems to me that this applies to our limited view of our own spiritual history. Perhaps we don't understand the principle of sisterhood because we have not looked closely enough at our past as women in the gospel of Jesus Christ. Perhaps that is where we should begin. Who are our female role models of the past? How did women express themselves in things of the spirit? What was their relationship with the Lord?

The sisterhood I am talking about is more than a female support group. It is more than our work as Relief Society sisters. It is an application of a higher principle that connects women with women, women with the Savior, and makes it possible for us to become consecrated to the things of the spirit in the lives we live.

In search of our spiritual roots, let's begin by looking at some of the women of the Old and New Testament. Considering the overwhelmingly antifemale bias that existed in Jewish culture, it is remarkable that we find any strong female models at all. But there are a few, and they are striking.

The book of Ruth provides us with a remarkable example of sisterhood in the lives of Ruth and Naomi. Ruth, a young, strong, and handsome woman, pledged her love and loyalty to Naomi, her mother-in-law, after the death of Ruth's husband. When Naomi pled for her return to her own country, Ruth responded: "Whither thou goest, I will go; and where thou lodgest, I will lodge; thy people shall be my people, and thy God my God." (Ruth 1:16.)

This loyalty, steadfastness, and devotion to Naomi and her God prepared Ruth for the affection of Boaz, which resulted in her marriage and the conception of Obed, the father of Jesse, the father of David. What is striking is not only their loyalty to each other, but also the centrality of the God of Israel in their relationship. Ruth's devotion to Naomi was constant and their mutual love of the Lord was unconditional, as they clearly felt the Lord's love was for them. Their relationship with each other prepared them for a higher level of sisterhood with the Lord.

In the New Testament, it is significant to note that many of the most significant events in the life of the Savior were shared with women. Jesus' first appearance after the Resurrection was to Mary Magdalene, whom he commissioned to bear witness. When she presented this news to the eleven disciples, they refused to believe her because, according to Judaic law, women were not allowed to bear legal witness.

A powerful statement about the women disciples of Christ is found in a book called *Portrait of Jesus: The Life of Christ in Poetry and Prose:*

The prominence of women among Jesus' first devoted and loyal contemporaries is notable. They were drawn to him alike by their needs and by his masterful personality and message. They came for healing, for forgiveness, for power to lead a new life, and for his benediction on their children. The timid woman who touched the hem of his garment, and when found out, came in fear and trembling to thank him; the aggressive Canaanite woman who would not be put off by the fact that she was not Jewish; the women who provided for him out of their means; and the mothers whose children he took in his arms and blessed, . . . laying his hands upon them, are typical. There is no explaining how that first precarious movement of thought and life which Jesus started, with so much against it and, humanly speaking, so little for it, moved out into its world-transforming influence, without taking into account the response of womanhood to Jesus.

When they were sunk in sin, he forgave them.
When they were humiliated, he stood up for them.
When they suffered social wrongs, he defended them.
When they had abilities to offer, he used them.
And, when they became sentimental and effusive in
    their devotion to him, he stopped them.

A woman in the crowd raised her voice and said to him, "Blessed is the womb that bore you, and the breasts you sucked"; but he said, "Blessed rather are those who hear the word of God and keep it." (Peter Seymour, ed., *Portrait of Jesus: The Life of Christ in Poetry and Prose,* Kansas City: Hallmark Crown Publishing, 1972, p. 34.)

Throughout the New Testament, we find the Savior teaching women their value. His life provided a model for a higher level of spiritual consciousness that women could enjoy. Perhaps this knowledge of our spiritual origins and values can prepare us for a higher sisterhood with the Lord.

In our modern-day revelations, the twenty-fifth section of the Doctrine and Covenants provides us with a statement of our possibilities as women and sisters. In this revelation, the Lord speaks to Emma Smith, saying, "Thou shalt be ordained under his [Joseph Smith's] hand to expound scriptures, and to exhort the church, according as it shall be given thee by my spirit." He tells Emma that part of her ordination, accomplished through the laying on of hands, is to receive the Holy Ghost. As he adds, "thy time shall be given to writing, and to learning much," it is clear that Emma is admonished to study, write, and influence. Emma is also promised, "Thy husband shall support thee in the church." Thus, Emma is not only to comfort and assist the Prophet, but she is also to receive similar support from him in her calling.

Section 25 implies that while the responsibilities of Joseph and Emma did overlap somewhat, his major concern was to provide administrative leadership for the Church, and hers was to provide an important dimension of spiritual and intellectual sensitivity. Here we find a model of teaching and reaching out, another significant connection of women with the Lord and with each other.

Sisterhood was institutionalized when the Prophet organized the Relief Society under the priesthood. I find the statement of goals of the society, as recorded in the Relief Society history, very similar to the concerns and life of the Savior. It reads: "The main objective of the Society is the care of the needy, the sick, the helpless and the unfortunate—to visit the widow and the fatherless—to administer comfort and consolation as well as temporal relief of physical wants, to see that none are left to suffer . . . also, to care for the dying and the dead, to be at the bedside of the lonely ones when death is near, to robe the body neatly and properly for burial when all is over, and to perform those kindly deeds with tenderness and grace." (Cheryll Lynn May, "Charitable Sisters," in *Mormon Sisters,* Cambridge, Massachusetts: Emmeline Press, 1976, p. 227.)

Here we have an expression of love and caring for those in greater need than ourselves. It is an expression of sisterhood, women joining together to serve others in Christ. As demonstrated in the life of Christ, reaching out to the poor results in the outpouring of spiritual well-being, creating a power within.

The expressions of sisterhood in the lives of women in early Utah are probably best known to us. The circumstances of nineteenth-century frontier life certainly brought women close together in their efforts to survive the hostile environment, often resulting in unusual spiritual strength.

Maureen Ursenbach Beecher has explored the nature of the support systems of Mormon women during this early period in her paper "Sisters, Sister Wives, and Sisters in the Faith" (unpublished manuscript, p. 10). Talking about these bonding experiences, she says: "One of those elements most frequently overlooked is the emotional bonding which occurred among sister wives, the sort of support which would permit Maggie Shipp, having been unsuccessful at her first attempt to complete a medical degree in an eastern college, to care for the three children of her sister [wife], Ellis, while she worked on her degree and graduated. The scraped-together sums of money Maggie sent Ellis were almost her entire support, their husband, Milford Bard, being often away on missions or studying himself. Not until after Ellis's return did Maggie complete her own degree." Not only do we find here important bonding experiences between sister wives, but also a remarkable expression of personal sacrifice on the part of Maggie for Ellis. Her sensitivities and generosity made it possible for her to function on a higher level of sisterhood.

Were the women of the Church in earlier times more spiritual than the women of the Church today? Why does it seem more difficult to experience those expressions of compassion, of spiritual gifts? What are the differences?

Attempting to answer some of these questions, Carol Cornwall Madsen says: "The circumstances of Mormon life often left women alone for long periods of time, frequently necessitating their assuming traditional male responsibilities as providers and heads of households. Sharing the common realities of their female roles in a Mormon society—frequent pregnancies, precarious childbirths, socialization of their children, economic responsibilities, household management, and the care for the sick and dead—Mormon women wherever they lived developed networks of mutual support, companionship and affection." ("Early Mormon Sisterhood," unpublished manuscript, p. 1.)

The harshness of the environment and the isolation of their communities provided incentives for women to develop close relationships of support. For us, the modern women of the Church, our isolation is different. We live in self-sufficient nuclear families. Our technology and affluence isolate us from one another. Since we do not need each other to survive, our sisterhood is in jeopardy of being less significant.

I have mentioned only a few expressions of sisterhood that we find in our past. Even though the voices of women of spiritual strength have been infrequent, it seems to me that the message is clear. Sisterhood is an association of women, from Mother Eve to the present, who are connected through their commitment to the Lord. We have been strengthened and guided by the light of Christ. Sisterhood is the accumulation of personal power that comes with the presence of Christ in our lives. Beyond testimony, it enables us to reach out to each other to give and to be strong. It is the personal power of sure knowledge of who we are and why we are here. That identity is central to our lives. Sisterhood is a principle of unity and direction. It connects all women through Christ and brings women together in unconditional love and trust. It nourishes, it builds up, and it facilitates growth.

Most of us have experienced special bonding moments with other women. When the Spirit of the Lord permeates those relationships, we begin to understand the sisterhood that President Kimball was talking about.

A powerful contemporary expression of sisterhood in the highest sense is found in the life of a humble, frail nun, Mother Teresa. This devoted sister and disciple of Christ has devoted her life to help to assuage the suffering of others. In accepting the Nobel Peace Prize, she spoke of love and suffering interchangeably. Living so close to death, she understands the meaning of life and stands as a model for women everywhere.

Women joined together through their commitment to

Christ is not an abstract notion. It is the reality of our possibilities as individuals. To be able to meet our many responsibilities, we need support, love, and definition so that we can be greatly enriched by each other. It seems to me that there is an urgent need for us, as women, as people, to move to a higher level of spirituality. Because we bring a great diversity of genetic material and cultural background to the Church, our personal styles differ. But our commitment to humanity through Christ is the unifying theme that brings us together in sisterhood.

Sisterhood for women is just as important as brotherhood and priesthood are for men. If properly understood, it can make a difference in the way we live our daily lives. Women receive additional blessings of the priesthood through ordinances and governance, but priesthood receives additional blessings through sisterhood, which provides a special sensitivity to things of the mind and spirit.

Our goals are the same: to be able to return to the presence of the Father. We are all responsible for teaching the gospel of Jesus Christ and for the welfare of his children here on the earth, but our role assignments differ. Regardless of our socialization and our sexuality, there are other important differences between men and women. It is now scientifically documented by Dr. Paul Goldman at Harvard that there are demonstrable differences in the perceptions of men and women. As Virginia Woolf said in her book *A Room of One's Own,* "Men and women are different. What needs to be made equal is the value placed on those differences." Because women's work has been less visible throughout the centuries, does that mean it is valued less? Because women are less visible in the scriptures, does that mean we are less spiritual?

The Church, from the time of Christ's ministry down to the present, has had to deal with the confusion of cultural norms and doctrine. Much of the thinking about the role of women is the result of this confusion. We are very fortunate to be living in a time when a prophet of the Lord is making some important distinctions about what is doctrine and what is not. He tells us how to prepare.

Finally, for a partnership to work, there must be two strong, contributing members. I would hope that our understanding of the importance of a sisterhood through our Savior would result in a strong partnership with the priesthood in doing the work of the Lord. There has never been a time when the Church was more in need of the unique contribution men and women can make, working together. We know that man is not to be without woman nor woman without man, and this is not only in a sexual and familial sense, but on every level of interaction in the Church. We need to understand each other better. We need to be reminded of the uniqueness of each. A comfortable relationship in our work, in the wards, in the stakes, or on the general level, can result in a self-confidence and power not yet experienced.

Priesthood and sisterhood can strengthen and bless each other. In the context of Christ's model, it can provide us with a vehicle of understanding differences, resulting in a new strength. Priesthood and sisterhood in an equal partnership can help to facilitate President Kimball's admonition when he said: "Finally, dear sisters, may I suggest to you something that has not been said before or at least in quite this way. Much of the major growth that is coming to the Church in the last days will come because many of the good women of the world (in whom there is often such an inner sense of spirituality) will be drawn to the Church in large numbers. This will happen to the degree that the women of the Church reflect righteousness and articulateness in their lives and to the degree that they are seen as distinct and different—in happy ways—from the women of the world." (*My Beloved Sisters*, p. 44.)

This is just a beginning. When we fully understand our possibilities as women in a sisterhood with the Lord, our real contribution will begin.

Grethe Ballif Peterson is a graduate of Brigham Young University and studied at Radcliffe, the College of Southern Connecticut, and Harvard University. She has served in many capacities in the community and the Church.

Dare to Make
a Difference

BEVERLY CAMPBELL

hat joy is in my heart as I join with you in sharing our common bonds of belief and hope and sisterhood. Never before in our history has there been a greater need for women to involve themselves in the workings of our society. Never has there been a greater need for women to step forward and affirm their moral and social values. Never have there been more significant issues that will affect—for good or for ill—our families, our homes, and our abilities to exercise our free choice.

Yes, this is women's time. And it will require something—some action, some commitment, some reaching out—from each one of us. Afton Affleck, in her book *Love Is the Gift* (Bookcraft, 1977, pp. 142-43), relates a significant and touching moment in her life, which stands as a reminder to her of her need to reach out:

> I knew Grandma was dying. The grown-ups were inside her bedroom—the door was closed. I stood in the hallway outside Grandma's room, a desolate, bewildered little girl, looking out of a glass-paned door at a wintry world. Then I heard someone singing. It was Grandma. I can still hear her voice, strong and

melodious, coming to me down through the years. It was as though she was giving me a gift—not to me exclusively, but inclusively, a gift meant for all her posterity and for the whole world.

Have I done any good in the world today?
Have I helped anyone in need?
Have I cheered up the sad and made someone feel glad?
If not, I have failed indeed.
Has anyone's burden been lighter today
Because I was willing to share?
Have the sick and the weary been helped on their way?
When they needed my help was I there?

There are chances for work all around just now,
Opportunities right in our way.
Do not let them pass by, saying, "Sometime I'll try,"
But go and do something today.
'Tis noble of man to work and to give;
Love's labor has merit alone.
Only he who does something is worthy to live;
The world has no use for the drone.

Then wake up, and do something more,
Than dream of your mansion above;
Doing good is a pleasure, a joy beyond measure,
A blessing of duty and love.

As this haunting message echoes down from one generation to another, it reminds us gently, but firmly, that we *must* care, that we *must* give, that we *must* dare to reach out, that we *must* make a difference.

Return with me for a moment to our heavenly home. God the Father is explaining the plan of salvation. He tells us of the creation of the world. He offers us, his children, the privilege of life. He tells us of the role of Father Adam and of Mother Eve. He shows us the need for a mediator who will enable us to return to his presence. We hear him ask, "Whom shall I send?" We recognize the voice of our elder brother: "Here am I, send me."

With those words our elder brother, Jesus Christ, became

the first volunteer. Oh, what a glorious volunteer! Do you suppose that at that time we might also have volunteered to share the burden of our Savior by asking if we could have the privilege of being our brother's keeper?

In a conference talk, Elder Robert L. Simpson said: "Before the foundations of this earth were laid, a glorious decision was made allowing you and me to be our brother's keeper. By faith and service we would be able to achieve a degree of glory in the hereafter suited to our Christlike efforts and our Christlike attainments." ("Go and Do Thou Likewise," *Ensign*, July 1973, p. 22.)

President Joseph F. Smith defined the purpose and duties of the Relief Society: "I will speak of the Relief Society as one great organization in the Church . . . whose duty it is to look after the interests of all the women of Zion and of all the women that may come under their supervision and care, irrespective of religion, color or condition." (*Gospel Doctrine,* Deseret Book, 1939, pp. 386-87.) How could we begin to carry out that mandate it we are only "hearers of the word"?

So important is the need for us to make a personal commitment to the service of our fellowmen that President Spencer W. Kimball made it the theme of a message to Regional Representatives in April 1980. He said: "Recently we established the new consolidated schedule which is aimed at enriching family life even further, together with greater opportunity for individual and family gospel scholarship and for more Christian service. We are trying to provide more time and emphasis on Christian service, so that our example can be more powerful in the world and so that those who are so worthy of attention might get more attention than they sometimes have in the past." ("We Feel an Urgency," *Ensign,* August 1980, p. 3.) And in a message to the youth of the Church, President Kimball said: "The Lord does notice us, and he watches over us. But it is usually through another person that he meets our needs. Therefore, it is vital that we serve each other." ("President Kimball Speaks Out on Service to Others," *New Era,* March 1981, p. 47.)

I've been very fortunate in my life in that I've had opportunities to see firsthand the great works of individual women who started with no more than a desire to fill a need, to alleviate human suffering, to make the world a better place in which to live, to serve another. And they have, indeed, made some very real differences.

My first such experience with a "doer of the word" was a woman named Louise Lake, a great shining light who fought a gallant battle in a body ravaged with polio—a woman who doctors were sure would never live through the first days of her battle; a woman who doctors were sure would never move from her bed; a woman left immobile, divorced, alone to raise a young daughter; a woman who through sheer guts—and there is no other word for it—willed herself into a wheelchair, willed herself to care for her own personal needs, and when I met her as a young woman of eighteen, had willed that she would provide for her own needs. I remember that her first endeavor was making lampshades because she could still use her hands.

Louise used the special insight she gained from her own affliction to teach the handicapped at the LDS Hospital in Salt Lake City. As a Gleaner girl under her loving stewardship, I often accompanied her as she worked her magic with these people. She developed significant and important new techniques for rehabilitation. In fact, so effective was her work that in 1958 she was named as the first national handicapped American of the year by President Eisenhower. She was named to the President's Commission on Employment for the Physically Handicapped. She was asked to go to New York City by Dr. Howard Rusk, one of our outstanding leaders in the rehabilitation field, where she was director of volunteers in the Institute of Physical Medicine and Rehabilitation at New York University Medical Center. There she became one of the great lights in the rehabilitation world as she developed new techniques that worked.

Louise Lake became so sought after because of her expertise that she traveled, alone (except for the wheelchair), across the length and breadth of South America, preaching and teaching the gospel of rehabilitation. She encouraged the development of hand controls for cars so that the handicapped could drive and no longer be immobile. I'll never forget her delight when she demonstrated this "device of freedom" to my husband and me. Aware of the needs of the human spirit, she encouraged the design of beautiful clothes that could meet the needs of the handicapped. She led the fight for removal of architectural barriers.

Who was Louise Lake? A woman with time? A woman with no responsibilities? A woman for whom it was easy? No. She was a woman who cared and who translated that care into action. When she died, the lead paragraph in one news story of her death read: "It is possible to use one's own pain and suffering to better understand the needs of others. But it is a rare person who does so. Such a person was Louise Johnson Lake."

My first experience with another great woman who is literally changing the concept of the world as to how we deal with the needs of human suffering began at the Kennedy Center in Washington, D.C. As coordinating director of the Kennedy Foundation, I was responsible for the functioning of a major event called the International Scientific Symposium, the culmination of which was the presentation of awards in the fields of science, service, and humanities to great contributors on the world scene. It was a majestic and joyous evening. The concert hall was filled with women in lavish evening gowns. The crystal chandeliers glowed; the men looked wonderful in their black-tie apparel. Great stars sang and played, and the time came to present the award for service. It was to go to Mother Teresa of Calcutta. As her name was called, out of this audience came this incredibly tiny, frail woman in a simple cotton sari with blue trim. Her feet were clad in worn leather sandals. She spoke simply and significantly of the needs and suffering of the world. Some 3,200 people rose to their feet, tears streaming down their faces, clapping in awe and wonder at this great woman.

We are all familiar with the frightening, divisive, destructive civil wars that have raged in Ireland for far too many years. Individuals and nations have struggled with its violence and hate, based on religious beliefs, which have turned streets into battlefields and children into fighters who must somehow try to deal with the hate and death. Certainly, one woman could make no difference. Churches, nations, and popes have tried to make a difference. Millions of dollars have been spent. But one woman, sickened by the ongoing destruction of human bodies and souls, felt she must try. She went to her church with a plan to bring the women of the two fighting factions, the Catholics and Protestants, together. The church leaders felt that this would not be possible, that the situation was too volatile. Well, she went ahead. Ever Irish, she said, "I decided some of us will have to be fools for the Savior's sake."

She was eventually able to gather together a few women who agreed that they were willing to risk their personal reputations and put aside their prejudices (for they were both Catholic and Protestant) if there was even a glimmer of hope that their voices might be heard. They each personally rejected violence, whatever its objective; they recognized that the goals for a united Ireland could not be accomplished through such means.

After much discussion as to how they might reach out to the thousands of women in Ireland who they felt sure shared their beliefs, they decided the only thing to do was to try to bring these women together in a common cause. They realized the risk they were taking, for it was a risk of life and limb to speak out as women from different factions united together. Nonetheless, they took out an ad in the Belfast newspapers. This ad invited all women who were opposed to violence and who were dedicated to peace to attend a meeting where they could discuss possible ways to alleviate the problems of fear and hate and suspicion prevailing between the two groups. They said they wanted to organize a movement that would be called "Women Together." The ad advised that buses would take the women to a particular hall.

The fifteen organizing women were at the hall well before the appointed hour of 8:00 P.M. Everything was readied and in order. At eight o'clock the lights were turned up and the waiting began. The hall was empty. Not a single person was in the seats. At 8:05 no one had entered. At 8:10 no one had entered. The women huddled together in consternation and concern. How could there not be one woman in all of Belfast who shared their concern? They were ready to leave when at 8:15 the doors burst open. In rushed hundreds of women. The buses had had to be rerouted. A street had been closed off because of a bomb threat.

The meeting began, and the organizing women each took their turn to explain why they felt such a movement was necessary and what might be some of their first simple steps of outreach to one another. They explained that such steps could perhaps be a first bridge of trust; that through sharing experiences, they could open lines of communication. After this discussion, those in the audience were asked to comment, to make suggestions, to reaffirm if they felt the ideas presented might work. Silence fell upon the hall; you could feel the mutual mistrust, a mistrust bred by decades of fighting and fears and anxieties. At long last a woman from Catholic Falls stood and identified herself. In a tremulous voice she said, "I wish to shake hands with a woman from Protestant Sahankill." Again there was silence. Not a head turned. Not a person moved. After what seemed like forever, a woman in the back arose and in an equally tremulous voice said, "I am from Protestant Sahankill." Suddenly the audience was alive. People were standing. Hands were outstretched. Names were exchanged. As the meeting was called to order again, there were countless suggestions of how these programs might work.

That night in a glorious moment of outreach of the human spirit, "Women Together" was formed. Their mission: to create understanding by establishing trust through communication and sharing. How to begin? They felt that they first should bring Protestant and Catholic children together. Just together, that's all. They arranged picnics for them; they arranged playground sessions; they established youth clubs. They now arrange and sponsor mixed groups to go together on holidays. They provide emergency aid.

And the wonderful thing that is happening is that a bridge is being built. The children are learning to trust. And perhaps, just perhaps, not in this generation but the next, through love and understanding, peace will follow in Ireland. You might be interested to know that so great was the contribution of this group (which started with just one woman saying, "Some of us must be fools for the Savior's sake") that two women, one Catholic, one Protestant, were awarded the Nobel Peace Prize.

Right at this moment, one woman is causing state legislatures all over this country to change their attitudes and approaches to drunk drivers. Each year, thousands of people are killed and maimed unnecessarily, senselessly, because of our lax laws regarding drunk drivers. The change in these laws is so long overdue, so desperately needed, that it is appalling to think we have gone this long without doing something about it. The woman: Candy Lightner. Her motivation: On May 3, 1980, the Lightners' twin daughters were walking home from school. A driver, driving drunk (not for the first time), hit and killed one of these lovely young women. The funeral was held on May 7, and the day after, Candy Lightner called several of her friends together to see if there was something they could do.

Although they banded together, much of the public contact was left to Candy. She met with opposition everywhere she turned. She was advised by the learned leaders of her community and elsewhere that many had tried and all had failed—that it simply "couldn't be done." She felt that since we were talking about laws, she would need to talk to the legislators, that surely they would understand the needs and champion her cause. She talked; they didn't listen. In fact, many of the legislators would not even do her the courtesy of meeting with her in personal conversation.

Candy was undaunted. She thought, "If I can't reach the legislators, perhaps I can find a friend in the press who will tell my story." She went to the press and told them her story and then explained to them about the difficult time she was having reaching legislators. They ran the story. Not so surprisingly, soon after, her phone began to ring. The legislators were ready to listen. This is a fledgling movement; however, already there are chapters in most states called MADD (Mothers Against Drunk Drivers). Candy was also asked by President Reagan to head a blue-ribbon commission to look into this problem and recommend solutions.

Yes, one person can make a difference. All you have to do is care and dare. And as President Kimball has said: *"Do it."*

And so you say, "Yes, I do want to make a difference. I recognize a need and I want to make a commitment." But then you wonder what it's going to be like out there. Is it going to be easy? Is it going to be comfortable? Am I always going to fit in?

The answer is no! Those of you who dare to step forward and make your presence and voices heard will find you have to leave the safety and security of the four walls of your warm, safe home. It will not be like your loving church callings. You may be buffeted about by people and institutions and governments that are not disposed or designed to make it easy. As a rule, you will not feel welcome or comfortable at first. You will sit in councils where your views may not be accepted. You will enter arenas where you may be in the minority and your view may be unpopular.

Just remember, the path is well worn. There are many women before you who as individuals have inconvenienced themselves, have risked exposure to criticism and ridicule, and as a result have made a significant contribution to the welfare of mankind. And, oh, the rewards are great!

I think of the story of our own beloved Sister Belle Spafford. As you know, the Church has long maintained membership in the National Council of Women. Shortly after Belle Spafford was sustained as general president of the Relief Society, a letter came across her desk advising of the NCW's annual meeting to be held in New York City.

Now, Sister Spafford had attended these meetings before. She was aware of their agenda and the workings within the organization. Based on this previous experience, she prepared a statement of recommendation to go to President George Albert Smith. In this letter, she listed all the reasons for such a recommendation. Uncertain and trembling just a bit, Sister Spafford placed the paper on the prophet's desk. He carefully read her letter. In it she explained how costly the membership in this organization was. She described the humiliation occasionally experienced because her views and those of the Church often did not fall into the mainstream of the views of the membership. She ended by saying, "We don't get a thing from these councils."

The wise old prophet tapped the letter on his desk, put it down, laced his fingers together, and then, tipping back in his chair, looked at her with a disturbed expression. "You want to withdraw because you get nothing from it. Do you always think in terms of what you get? Don't you think in terms of what you have to give?" He returned the paper and with considerable firmness said, "You continue your membership in these councils and make your influence felt."

Needless to say, she did continue her membership, and with love and quiet understanding of others' needs, she made her influence felt. The day came when Sister Spafford was elected national president of that organization. She had long served on their executive board both at a national and international level and was recognized as one of the great women of and most important contributors to that organization.

Now, you don't have to take on the world. And it isn't always going to be combative. There are thousands of needs that must be met and thousands of ways in which to meet them. All you have to do is love your fellowman; be concerned for the welfare of someone or something—your home, your family, the educational systems, taxes, women's issues, community, state or national government, the symphony, the arts program in your community. Whatever your interest, whatever your talent, whatever your concerns, there is a need for you, a place for you, and a program that wants you.

You can join an organized group, or you can see a need and form an ad hoc group to meet that need. You can join a political party and help to bring changes in that forum. You can run for office or help others run for office. You can join a commission or organize a commission. You can work as an individual or on a one-to-one basis. The choices are endless. The important thing is, you are needed, and we each must do something if we are to maintain a society and a form of society that will reflect our values and meet the real human needs that exist.

Yes, we do need to be about our Father's business. I am

haunted by that song's stern admonition: "Only he who does something is worthy to live." And this means being *in* the world, interacting with, responding to, caring for, and contributing to the lives of our fellowmen. We may be different from, but we should not falsely stand apart from, our fellowman.

One word of caution: As you step out into that world, you must be sure your own testimony is in good repair. You must have examined your heart and found the chinks in your own armor so that you will be able to withstand the pressures and the advancement of false ideas and values that may come your way.

As you enter that larger world, you must fortify yourself by holding up to the test of eternal truths each and every social issue for which you are going to work. The pendulum swings, attitudes change, social needs come and go, social causes wax hot and cold, but eternal truth is eternal truth, and all programs must be examined in that light.

A good example of this is the current so-called woman's movement. Ten, five, even two years ago, the headlines, the articles, the books all screamed at us that the only satisfaction and fulfillment for women was outside of the home. We all had to have careers if we were to be fulfilled and if we did not, we were somehow denigrated, downtrodden, enslaved. We are discovering that the noted newsman Marvin Kalb was tellingly prophetic when he said: "We have no valid evidence that today's headlines will be tomorrow's wisdom. Undoubtedly, some of the things for which women are clamoring today will be in the discard tomorrow." How true this is.

Some time ago one of the leading feminists wrote an article for the *Washington Post* called "Superwoman—Super Tired." In it she asked, "Is what women got what women want?" She talked about the fact that she had looked at her mother at home all day, seemingly going from one rote task to another, as unfulfilled. Now she wonders if her own daughter, who had seen her rushing to and fro from work to home, never having enough time for herself or her family, will look at her in pity and call her unfulfilled.

In an article in *The Washington Monthly,* Deborah Fallows

talked about the myth of the "successful woman." She said, "I'm glad to be part of a generation of women who are free to make choices about careers and families. However, as far as I can tell, the seamless web of family and prestigious career just doesn't work. At some point, you have to sit down and decide whether to conduct your life in pursuit of money, status, power, or something else. The something else is hard to describe because it's not part of the official story of my generation of women. But I know it's there."

Susan Gibson, who teaches English at a Virginia college, wrote in the *Washington Post* an article entitled "What's That Again? Feminism?" She said:

> The old days were the early '70s when I was single, in graduate school, poor, independent, fervent, intellectual and feminist. These days I am married, working and mothering, affluent, and my life is entwined inextricably with my husband and my child; my colleagues, my students, my child's caregiver, doctors, neighbors, bands and so on. Independent? I can't go down to High's without putting the clothes in the dryer and finding the baby's car strap and making sure the back door is locked.
>
> Feminism did not prepare me for marriage and childbirth. Contrary to what I'd believed, after the initial shock, I loved pregnancy. And I loved my baby. Loved is hardly the word for it; for a year or more I was possessed. . . . I find myself concerned about a generation of children brought up outside a home and determined to be home a great deal. I find myself looking at baby boys and baby girls and seeing differences. I have come into a sense that masculinity and femininity are complex and deep-seated, not accidents of the physical surface. I want another child.

Yes, the pendulum swings. And we must measure all our actions, all our commitments to social programs, all our comings and goings with the eternal truths.

Indeed, you are fortunate in that you do have the choice to do whatever it is in life that you feel you must do. However, you must weigh these choices against eternal truths and not be swayed by the pressures of popular causes or the headlines heralding the rhetoric of the so-called modern woman.

In this same vein, you must dare to be spiritually strong. Sister Elaine Cannon has reminded us time and again that "like our brethren, we too have a mighty errand of our own." President Kimball has told us that "much of the major growth that is coming to the Church in the last days will come because many of the good women of the world . . . will be drawn to the Church in large numbers." He goes further, saying, "Thus it will be that the female exemplars of the Church will be a significant force in both the numerical and the spiritual growth of the Church in the last days." (*My Beloved Sisters,* pp. 44, 45.)

More than spiritually strong, we must become spiritual giants. That is what the Lord expects of us. President Heber C. Kimball said: "It is not only the privilege but the *solemn duty* of every Latter-day Saint woman, married or unmarried, to cultivate the spiritual powers that lie within her own soul. The time is coming when no man or woman will be able to endure on borrowed light. Each will have to be guided by the light within himself. If you do not have it, you will not stand."

We also must become capable, effective, even great leaders, for in these last days there will be such growth in the Church and such need for our leadership both within and outside the Church that without every woman exercising her full leadership potential, we will be found wanting, and the growth of the Church will be hampered.

And finally, my dear sisters, you must dare to like yourself and dare to be yourself. Too often as I travel about this great church and talk to women's groups, I find them carrying enormous burdens of guilt and expressing a great sense of unease because they are not living up to all that they feel they should be doing. They feel great anxiety because they feel they are not fitting perfectly into the "typical Mormon woman" mold. They wonder what is wrong with them. In fact, they nearly always say to me, "But you're not the typical Mormon woman either." I generally ask the questioner what a typical Mormon woman is and nearly always am advised that it is a woman who stays home all the time, has many children, bakes bread, cans fruit, and sews her children's clothes. Now these are all valid and worthy functions of Mormon women, but does a Mormon woman have to do *all* these or can she do other things that she does better and more happily, but that still bring about the desired end?

Would it not be better to say that a typical Mormon woman is one who has an enormous reverence for life and the bearing and nurturing of children? That she places great value on a warm and inviting home? That her husband and family come first? That she has the ability to refine and conserve the family's resources? Would she not then just as well fit the mold? Would we not be better able to understand ourselves and articulate our lives if we thought of the typical Mormon woman in these *value* terms rather than the beforementioned *task* terms? I think so. And I want you from this moment on to regard yourself in these value terms.

I want you to place value on your endeavors and your uniqueness. I counsel you that fear and guilt are harmful, that they immobilize you and use energy which you cannot spare. In the words of Emerson: "Finish each day and be done with it. You have done what you could. Some blunders and absurdities no doubt crept in—forget them as soon as you can. Tomorrow is a new day. Greet it well and serenely, and with too high a spirit to be cumbered with your old nonsense."

And in all this you will be whole, you will be fortified, you will be prepared to do the Lord's work, to fulfill the commitments you made in the councils of heaven—to be your brother's keeper.

Oh, and what a difference you will make! As Robert Kennedy said, "Few will have the greatness to bend history itself, but each of us can work to change a small portion of events, and in the total of all those acts will be written the history of this generation."

I beg of you, become involved. Join the women's commissions, the study groups, the task forces. Let your voice be heard in the social service agencies, the educational institutions, the White House conferences; and then carry the message to your sisters and to your brothers. I often think of the haunting Civil War song that tells the story of two little brothers playing on their stick horses. Johnny breaks his horse and begins to cry. Jack, who has dashed ahead, turns around and gallops back. As he comforts his little brother, the song goes: "Did you think I would leave you crying when there's room on my horse for two? Come on, John, we'll soon be flying. I can go just as fast with you." Years pass and the brothers grow to manhood. The Civil War comes and both young men go off to war. But one is wearing a uniform of blue, the other a uniform of gray. One day they meet in fierce battle. Jack falls from his horse wounded. Without hesitation, John gallops out onto the battlefield, leaps from his mount, and kneels to cradle his brother's head in his arms, saying, "Did you think I would leave you dying, when there's room on my horse for two? Come on, Jack, we'll soon be flying. I can go just as fast with you."

Are we who believe that we have a clearer view of the history of this country, of its constitution, of man and his destiny, to leave our fellowmen crying? Or shall we involve ourselves in those issues of greatest concern to us all? For is it not also true that none is free while one remains discriminated against or disadvantaged in whatever way?

How great is woman's role! How proud I am to be a woman, a Mormon woman, a member of The Church of Jesus Christ of Latter-day Saints. I am who I am because of my church. I have the confidence to try because I know I am a child of God, because I know that he cares for me in most singular and infinite ways.

Beverly Campbell is president of a public relations firm in the Washington, D.C., area. She has been a counselor to the Eastern Seaboard Public Communications Council and active in community and church service.

The Savior:
An Example for Everyone

KAREN LYNN DAVIDSON

*I*n talking about the Savior, perhaps the place to start is by recalling the announcement of his birth. Those unsuspecting shepherds who thought they were in for just another cold winter's night watching some sleepy sheep must have been very surprised when the angel appeared to them and announced: "Behold, I bring you good tidings of great joy, which shall be to all people." (Luke 2:10.) The announcement of those good tidings is fairly straightforward—"Behold, I bring you good tidings of great joy"—but why do you suppose the angel needed to add, "which shall be to all people"? Is it possible that the angel added those words because at that moment the shepherds needed some reassurance? Perhaps they were afraid that the angel had made a mistake, that these blessings were not really meant for lowly shepherds; but the angel stipulated without any ambivalence that the tidings were for *all people.*

Think for a moment how in those times so few things would have been for all people. In those times people took for granted that different groups had different laws, privileges, and customs; in fact, virtually nothing accrued to you simply because you had been born and existed as a human being. That is quite a modern idea. Society's assumptions about you and your assumptions about your-

101

self would have depended on your race, your sex, and the class you had been born into. Nothing, until the Savior's announcement, was really for all people. And while some may think otherwise, the Savior never added a footnote to his life or to his list of teachings that said, "By the way, everything that I have done and everything that I have said is relevant to only 48 percent of the population; the other 52 percent will have to look someplace else to find the way, the truth, and the light, because what I have said and what I have done are not relevant to women." Instead, he came to teach all people, both men and women, the kind of life our Father in heaven would have us lead.

Yet often, sometimes without even realizing it, we women hear certain of the Savior's teachings and we think that while it is a beautiful message, it doesn't apply to us, or at least not very forcefully. I would even guess that nearly every woman has at some time, in some way, excused herself from really responding to the admonitions of the Savior, simply because she is a woman. What a tragedy it is to think that the one perfect life that was ever lived, the one infallible example that we have, the one teacher we have as to what to do with our earth life, is somehow not fully for us.

Some may have a hard time believing that they do this. You may be thinking to yourself, "Maybe I don't live a perfectly Christlike life, but I don't use the fact that I'm a woman as an excuse for my shortcomings." I am sure that our rejection of the full responsibility of a Christlike life is rarely quite this conscious or this deliberate, but some things may be happening that are difficult to recognize. Those subtle rejections are what I would like to examine—some of the ways we as women consciously or unconsciously decline the responsibility of living a fully Christlike life.

As we look at what the scriptures tell us about the Savior's life, we see a personage of many facets. One side of his behavior is the side that is most often represented in verse, in music, and in paintings—the gentle side of Christ. He could shed tears, he could bless little children, he could be kind to someone who had been rejected by every other person. He rejected the worldly notions of dominion, power, and bosshood. On the other hand, no one who has ever lived has shown more strength, more courage, more perseverance, more willingness to stand up for truth or rebuke wrong, even at tremendous cost, than has the Savior. He spoke up for unpopular causes. He was willing to speak the truth, even when it cost him his life. If his inner inspiration told him something was right, he did it. That confirmation was all he needed. He didn't need an okay from any of his friends. He had the strength to stand alone. He had absolute confidence in himself and in his Father—confidence to lead out in what was right.

It is this side of the Savior's character—the side that grows, helps others to grow, leads, speaks out, and seeks first and foremost the approval of his Father—that too many women ignore. Many women assume, without really thinking about it, that this part of the Savior's example really has nothing to do with them.

But what on earth would cause a woman to decide that half of Christ's attributes were not relevant to her? Her Creator didn't give her a second-rate mind or second-rate talents. No General Authority ever told her to act weak or simple-minded or incompetent. The scriptures do not tell her that she is less than a whole person. What is the source of this dreadfully destructive message? What would cause a woman to shy away from the full responsibility of a Christlike life by saying, "These things are beyond what I'm expected to do. These teachings are not meant for me because I know I could never measure up"?

The fact is that we don't have to look too far. We are surrounded every day by influences that teach women these untruths. How happy Satan must be when he sees women, particularly Latter-day Saint women, absorbing day by day the idea that we are incompetent, unreliable, unimaginative, and unimportant. The sources of these lies are numerous, but I would like to mention briefly three sources that suggest to women that it is all right to accept the gentle side of Christ's example but not the strong side.

The first important and pervasive negative influence is one that none of us escaped. Those who are involved in elementary education or who have studied children's literature can bear me out, as can some recent scholarly studies. This first villain is many aspects of our school experience, particularly the elementary school textbooks we learned to read from. (Textbooks are gradually improving in reflecting girls and women with more dignity and in a more interesting way, but the ones we learned from are almost certain to have done us damage.) When children read these books, what do they see boys doing? The boys invent things. They go on hikes. They take care of animals. They talk about what they want to be when they grow up. What do the girls tend to do in these stories? The girls watch the boys. They admire them. They make food and serve it to the boys. They go shopping for new dresses and do other things that will make them pretty, and they help their mothers.

One study showed that in stories where one sex demeans the other, out of sixty-seven stories, the little boys demeaned the little girls in sixty-five. In two out of the sixty-seven, the little girls demeaned the little boys. Girls are pictured in children's books only one-half as often as boys and are main characters of the stories only one-fourth as often. And the thing that really hurts is that when the little girls are the main characters in the story, they don't *solve* the problems presented in the story; they *are* the problems presented in the story. Usually they have to be rescued by their fathers or their big brothers or even their little brothers.

Regarding classroom experience other than with textbooks, let me refer to a recent study on teacher-student interaction in the elementary school classrooms: "It appears that the types of behavior which elicit teacher feedback in elementary classrooms differ for boys and girls. Boys receive most of their negative feedback for nonacademic behavior—making noise—and most of their positive feedback for academic performance. Girls are most likely to receive negative feedback for their academic work and positive feedback for nonacademic behavior, namely being neat. Differences in teacher-student interaction patterns may contribute to sex differences in students' beliefs regarding the causes of their successes and failures and in their willingness to take on new challenges. Girls are likely to attribute their failures to lack of ability and their successes to hard work. Boys are likely to attribute their failures to lack of hard work and their successes to their own abilities." That is a crucial distinction. A little girl who is brought up under the influence of these messages from textbooks and these inter- actions in the classroom is being told that somehow she intrin- sically just doesn't have what it takes to follow the Savior's pat- tern. She is not strong. She is not courageous. She is not resourceful or dependable. She is not important for herself, as a person. She is not active. In all these ways, she is being told that, because she is female, she lacks or had better learn to pre- tend to lack these qualities, because that's how girls are.

The second negative influence is advertising. Although some advertisers are becoming much more conscious of the way in which they may be demeaning the role of women, it is impossible not to sense the negative impact of the image of women in most advertisements. What is the role of women in most TV advertisements? The woman is shown in very limited roles, usually in very limited locations—mainly the kitchen and the bathroom. She is full of problems, again, just like the little girls in the elementary school readers. Often it is a rather sim- ple problem centered on the kitchen or the laundry, but the problems have her so baffled that many times a man must enter and offer a solution.

The newspaper columnist Carrie Beauchamp recently dis- cussed the unfortunate role representations in the media:

> Television commercials are the worst offenders, com- pounding the role model of subservient female with the subliminal message of the authoritative male voice. Time and again we are hit with variations of the same theme [of the] hopeless, insecure female being directed and reas- sured by the off-camera man who knows all. I might not be so offended by these scenes, if there was any hope that the man knew anything about the subject at hand. Just once, I would love to see one of those men get in front of the camera, bend over the tub, and scrub that ring out himself. The latest trend in commercials is the spontane- ous woman-on-the-street interview, which then cuts to a

similar interview with her husband. It was bad enough when wives were being embarrassed in front of God, their mothers-in-law, and the world for not knowing what they should have discussed before they were married right along with how many children they wanted—that he would prefer stuffing to potatoes—but now women are being barraged with a new level of guilt for not knowing that men notice the softness in clothes. After blushing with embarrassment, the wife is asked in the most condescending tones by that off-camera voice: "Now, what brand of softener will you buy next time?" It is as if she were a three-year-old who will learn only by repeating the brand name aloud fifty times. . . . It is hard enough to survive as a wife, mother, and worker in this society. Credits are few and far between and self-respect hard enough to maintain without adding new burdens like buying the right clothes softener.

The women shown in advertisements often appear shallow, preoccupied with short-term goals. Most of them do not leave the impression of being concerned with eternal goals or the significant pressures of life. By implication, these more profound questions are left to men. It would be very difficult to overestimate the harm of these influences that we and our sisters and our daughters are subjected to almost every day. Instead of being pictured as someone who is concerned with deep family problems, someone who is capable of seeking the virtues and achievements of a Christlike life, the woman in the advertisement is thrown into a crisis for fear her mother-in-law will see that the dishwasher left spots on the crystal.

The third influence is that of movies and television. Although in real life many women devote themselves unselfishly to important kinds of service and to high ideals, movies and especially television almost never reflect this fact. Instead, whether it is comedy or more serious drama, women are shown as selfishly seeking their own advantage or as asking approval from others in a very shallow way. These women are either cunning and manipulative, trying to obtain their own goals, or childishly dependent.

In addition, the main female characters of movies and television are almost always young and attractive, attributes not necessarily true of the main male characters. Many older actors can play a romantic lead in a film, but almost always the main female characters are young and attractive, leaving women who do not fit this image with a lesser view of their own worth. When Brooke Shields appeared on the cover of *Time* magazine, she was fourteen years old. The cover article described her as "the female figure that women in the United States now want to look like." Can you imagine women wanting to look like a fourteen-year-old? These young and attractive women are the ones who are admired and the ones people pay money to see. No other women seem worthy of this attention.

What kind of a Christlike view of herself can a woman have when every day she is told that she is not important unless she is beautiful and charming—that women tend to be shallow and selfish and worth only what their physical appearances or their underhanded manipulations can gain for them? Again, Satan must rejoice when he sees women told again and again, "This is all you are; this is all you are worth." The confidence, the outward reach that anyone, man or woman, must have in order to make the first steps toward godhood are certainly not compatible with this very low-minded view of women conveyed by the media.

I would now like to discuss the Savior's most important teachings meant for all people, and I want to suggest that some women do not take these teachings seriously. The first of the three messages I have chosen is that any individual is of worth, that every human being is important—bond or free, Greek or barbarian, male or female. The shepherd leaves the ninety and nine to go after the one. Heaven rejoices when one single soul is saved. Do you accept this teaching that every human being is of infinite worth in terms of yourself? Let me list just a few negative ways of thinking, because I want to suggest that if any of these assumptions reflect your view of yourself, you have demeaned yourself and have accepted a less than full vision of yourself.

1. If you feel that your worth depends on being young and physically attractive, you have in a sense rejected the Savior's

teachings about the intrinsic worth of every human being. You have also set the stage, I think, for a very difficult life for yourself. One of my students recently went into the closet for her twenty-first birthday. She simply was not going to tell anyone that she was turning twenty-one. Already she was withdrawing because she was worried about her age. Doctors' offices and clinics are full of women who cannot cope with the trauma of their thirtieth or their fortieth or their fiftieth birthday. Because of external and relatively unimportant reasons, they have lost their feelings of self-worth. Can you imagine the Savior withholding his love from an elderly or less attractive woman? Yet we do not make the same allowances for ourselves. I hope that Latter-day Saint women will know that their essential worth and the things important to them are not tied up with their age or attractiveness.

2. If you convey to any woman—to yourself, your mother, your roommate, your sister, your daughter, or your girl friend—a message that just because she is a woman, certain skills and professions and achievements are beyond her capacity, you have labeled her unfairly. You have told her that she is a member of a second-class group. The Savior never told her that. You have not truly recognized her as an individual, and you have missed the point of one of the Savior's most important teachings. You have steered her away from the possibility of a fully Christlike life because you were not seeing her individual, unique worth.

3. If, because you are a woman, you hold back from accepting leadership positions, from speaking up in class, or from doing the best work you are capable of, you have not really accepted yourself as a person of dignity and importance and ability. I am sorry to report that at BYU we have thousands of women students who are dabblers as far as their school work is concerned—also a few men who fall into that category, but more women than men by far. Tithing funds are supporting them in this dabbling, and I feel that the day will come when they will be held responsible for the waste of these sacred tithing funds. It is a tragic human waste, and it is a tragic finan-

cial waste. If a woman has a vision of her own individual worth, she will not dabble.

4. If you find yourself having to define yourself in terms of someone else, you have not really understood what the Savior meant by dignity and individual worth. Every woman, married or single, must be able to define herself in terms of herself and not in terms of her relationship or lack of relationship with someone else. The prophets have stressed many times that marriage is an appropriate and universal goal. But it has been my observation that the best marriages, the best engagements, are not the results of directly seeking after marriage. The best marriages seem to be a by-product of pursuing many different kinds of worthy goals. In other words, a young woman at Brigham Young University or anywhere else who devotes her full attentions and energies to finding a husband may well find one, but this perhaps will not be the best kind of match. The best marriage will be the one that comes when the young woman is not so much concerned with finding the right one as with *being* the right one.

When Harold B. Lee first saw the woman who was to become Freda Joan Lee, she was wheeling her crippled stepfather into sacrament meeting in a wheelchair. Now it would be my guess that many women would have liked to sit in ambush for that very, very eligible widower, handsome Harold B. Lee. I imagine there were women who were contriving to sit by him in church or to bring by a little bottle of jam. I imagine there were women who were buying new dresses in hopes that he would notice them, but the ambush tactics did not work. What did work was that the future Sister Lee was doing what she was supposed to. Without exception, the presidents of the Church have chosen for their wives women who have a sense of their own worth, who have made their mark before they were married, and who continued to make a mark after they were married.

If a woman devotes her total energies and time and talents to getting married, then she is not inclined to see herself in terms of her individual worth. She has defined herself only in terms of someone else. She does not understand what the Savior taught about individual worth. If you are single or if you are married, do not wait for someone else to make you happy. Do not wait for someone else to bring you forward. Do not wait for someone else to enable you to do important things during this life. The Savior taught that you are important just for yourself, not just as you are defined in terms of someone else.

Another of the Savior's crucial teachings is that of service. The way we show our love for him is through serving others, because when we serve others, he has told us, we are serving him. We all acknowledge the importance of service within the home; unfortunately, many women do not see in themselves the additional capacity for large-scale service outside the home. But the Church cannot afford to give up half of its leadership just because women might decide it is more appropriate to hang back and pretend that they won't or can't serve. We must have leaders, both men and women. We must have women who are willing to rebuke error and wrong and to speak up for moral standards that we as Latter-day Saints know are right.

The early sisters of the Church never thought of acting simple-minded and incompetent or of coasting along inconspicuously in the Church. Before they joined the Church, they were bound by the horrible limitations of supposedly proper Victorian womanhood. They were to be submissive, pure, pious, and domestic—which are all fine qualities, but that was the ceiling. Those teachings of society told them they were subservient, a piece of furniture, someone's possession, only an ornament. But after their conversion, they were free. They learned something different about themselves. When Joseph Smith organized the Relief Society, he stated specifically that the sisters were responsible for their own sins, for their own salvation, and for their own spiritual gifts. Women such as Eliza R. Snow nd Emmeline B. Wells knew they were needed badly, so they served. Is the need of the Church any less now for us? Shouldn't our beliefs help to keep us from the kinds of influences we looked at earlier?

It is not just the Church that needs the leadership and influence of *all* the righteous people—there is a whole world out there badly in need of voices to speak out for right causes. In one respect the Church does not have a very good reputation in the world: we do not have a good reputation for supporting righteous community and national causes. Our excuse usually is that we are too busy with our church assignments. I am not sure that excuse will do in all cases. Can we really ignore the millions of our nonmember brothers and sisters who need us? There are many who never join the Church in this life, but they still need us. They need what we know. Imagine what examples we could be. Imagine how many people could be drawn to the Church if we would lend our strengths and talents to the needs of our communities, such as the need to eliminate child abuse and child alcoholism, the need for righteous leadership on school boards, the need for community youth leadership, the need to assist lonely, elderly people as well as the underprivileged of the world.

As we think about helping in these causes and lending our service and talents outside our Church, we should be prepared to do more than just flutter in and say, "Here I am; what can I do to help?" It is much better to go in and say, "Here I am; let me tell you about my skills. I am a nurse (or an accountant, or a lawyer, or an artist, or a writer, or I have had administrative experience). I have very conspicuous parenting skills. I have a degree in home economics; therefore, I am especially qualified to go on a health mission." Have the skills, not just the willingness. When we see a wrong, let's be capable of more than just indignation. Let's be skilled enough to express our indignation in a way that will convince other people and then be able to suggest and carry out some solutions. As President Harold B. Lee said, "It's good to be faithful; it's better to be faithful and competent."

We have been talking about service outside the home, but I do not think that being skilled and alert and competent is likely to make anyone a worse mother. I think it is likely to make someone a much better mother. I know because I am the daughter of such a mother, and I think that those who are also the daughters of such mothers will agree that we can count this as one of the greatest blessings of our lives. So in the home as well as outside the home, the ideal of service is important. Conspicuous and significant kinds of service that will serve as a beacon to many people are the results of our preparing ourselves with the skills to perform them.

Another critical teaching of the Savior is that of eternal progression. "Be ye therefore perfect, even as your Father which is in heaven is perfect." (Matthew 5:48.) The doctrines of the Church do not refer to people in the hereafter as "kings and clinging vines" or as "gods and shrinking violets." Instead, we learn of "priests and priestesses, gods and goddesses." The Savior taught that both men and women must move forward in the development of spirituality, that all must seek wisdom and knowledge. President Harold B. Lee said, "The gospel has nothing to do with being. The gospel has only to do with becoming." Yet how many people—and again, I think, particularly women—are content just to *be* instead of to *become,* to be passive, to wait, to react just as they have been taught through textbooks and the media, instead of planning their own growth and working on it steadily. It is not enough to say, "Oh, my husband is doing wonderfully, my children are doing wonderfully." I hope the woman who speaks these words is also doing wonderfully, because no one else's growth can substitute for her own.

We have looked at three of the Savior's most important teachings—individual worth, service, and eternal progression. We have also mentioned that his life took in many facets. One side was gentle; it was the side that women find the most natural role model, at least at first glance. One side was very strong and effective. Let me conclude just by listing four points that I think will be true of a woman who truly accepts the Savior as an example in her life.

First, if a woman truly accepts the Savior as her example, she will, when she sees in the world a need for service or expertise, train for that service and then make the finest possible contribution as a professional or volunteer within the context of her other responsibilities.

Second, if a woman truly accepts the Savior as her example, she will accept his teachings concerning individual worth and dignity. She will see herself as a unique person, not subject to someone else's idea of the role she should play. She will find what is right for her and allow other women the same flexibility. There is no one way for a woman to be. We can each be very different. Different things can be important to us, and that is all right.

Third, if a woman truly accepts the Savior as her example, she will not accept the world's false limitations, the handcuffs that printed materials or broadcast materials would place upon her. These false messages serve the purposes of Satan. The serious work of the world and the responsibility for being competent belong to women too.

Fourth, if a woman truly accepts the Savior as her example, she will seek principally for his approbation and validation. She will not let her happiness or feeling of self-worth depend on other human beings whose vision may be helpful on the one hand, but whose vision possibly may be limited, on the other hand, by some of these pervasive false influences that we have been talking about.

To know that we are daughters of our Father in heaven should give us a tremendous sense of joy but also a tremendous sense of responsibility. I hope we can say to ourselves, "I am the daughter of my Father in heaven. As his daughter, I know that I am important because I am me. I know I am capable of great growth, capable of significant service. I will not cancel myself in any way by yielding to false influences that tell me that I am a shallow being or a being of lesser worth or lesser ability. I know that the Savior's examples and teachings were to all people. I will please my Father in heaven by taking his daughters seriously."

Karen Lynn Davidson received a doctorate from the University of Southern California and was director of the honors program and associate professor of English at Brigham Young University. She also served as a member of the general Church music committee.

Within Whispering
Distance of Heaven

PATRICIA T. HOLLAND

t is about family challenges that I wish to speak, and I especially wish to speak to mothers and mothers-to-be. We ask ourselves, "Can it be done? Can we raise a righteous family in an increasingly difficult world?" We search for answers everywhere—in psychology books, in child development courses, and even from Erma Bombeck. We run ourselves ragged because we want straight A's and straight teeth. We panic that we are doing too much for our children and then get a headache worrying that we're not doing enough. We even get caught in the crunch of choosing between family duties and church callings when both need our loyalty and both need our devotion.

We especially feel anxious as our babies grow into teenagers. Sometimes it's hard to see them becoming independent young men and women, and we fear we'll lose those relationships that made us feel so secure when they were in the cradle. Some in our neighborhoods experience these struggles all alone as single parents. And as if these problems weren't enough, we have to face them along with the fact that our hair is graying, our tummies are bulging, and our energies are sagging. Occasionally, we, as parents, would like to run away from home too, but we can't get the keys to the car.

Humor aside, we know how serious our task is. We are, after all, the generation raised on the admonition that no success can compensate for failure in the home. The weight of that statement often seems more than we can bear, but I have come to realize that anything very important is weighty and difficult. Perhaps the Lord designed it that way so that we would cherish and retain and magnify the treasures that matter the most. Like the seeker in the parable, we too must be willing to go and sell all that we have for those pearls of great price. Our families, along with our testimonies and loyalty to the Lord, are the most prized of all such pearls. I think you'll agree that they are worth some agony and anxiety. To have life go along easily might mislead us in time and leave us ill prepared for eternity.

I also believe that with the task is also given the talent. Like Nephi, I do not believe God will ask us to do anything without preparing the way for us to accomplish it. We are his children, and we must never forget that fact—in joy or in sorrow. And with the additional help we can receive through the veil, we are able to say with the angels, "Is any thing too hard for the Lord?" (Genesis 18:14.)

I have taken great comfort in that scripture over the years. It is, as you may recognize, a family-oriented scripture. It is the scripture at the heart of everything we now call the seed of Abraham, Isaac, and Jacob.

In our early married life, it appeared as if I too, like Sarah, would be barren. My doctor told us there was a good chance we would have no children; but in my heart I felt otherwise, and I remembered Sarah. "Is any thing too hard for the Lord?" No, not if their names are Matt, Mary Alice, and Duffy. Is it too hard to conceive them, or bear them, or nurse them, or comfort them, or teach them, or clothe them, or wait up for them, or be patient with them, or cry over them, or love them? No, not if we remember that these are God's children as well as ours. Not if we remember those maternal stirrings that are, I suppose, the strongest natural affections in the world.

President David O. McKay said once that the nearest thing to Christ's love for mankind is a mother's love for her child. Everything I have felt since June 7, 1966, tells me he was right.

When troubles come (and they will), when challenges mount (and they will), when evils abound and we fear for our children's lives, think of the covenant and promise given to Abraham and especially think of Sarah. And with the angels we should ask ourselves, "Is any thing too hard for the Lord?" If we think circumstances in our lives are not ideal, we can take heart. I'm beginning to wonder if circumstances are ever ideal. Let me use my own life as an example.

Because of various educational opportunities and professional assignments that have come to us, we have moved fourteen times in seventeen years of marriage. When the children started to come, those moves were an increasing concern to me. I worried about the children adjusting and settling in and finding friends. Their emotional safety through our very busy lives has caused me a great, great deal of concern.

When we were in graduate school with two small children, the student housing that we lived in was on the edge of the black community in New Haven, Connecticut. Almost all the other parents in that area either put their children in private schools or jumped district boundaries. But because we couldn't afford a private school and because we felt it dishonest to jump boundaries, Matt was literally the only white boy in his kindergarten class and one of two white children in the entire school.

I can still remember the tears and the terror. This is my firstborn, the treasure of my life. He was the boy on whom I had practiced all my child development courses. He was the child I had taught to read before he was three years old, and I was certain he was destined to become one of the legendary greats of western civilization. How could his educational beginnings, his first stirrings from the warmth and protection of the nest, be so startling, so much to adjust to? But I remembered then, and I remember now, something George Bernard Shaw once said: "I don't believe in circumstances. The people who get on in this world are the people who get up and look for the circumstances they want, and if they can't find them, make them." (*Mrs. Warren's Profession,* act 2.) Clinging to the hope that maybe this was one of those opportunities for growth, and fighting to control my fears, I threw myself into the PTA. I also volunteered to provide the school's music training once a week. Well, that was one year, which seems so very long ago. A great deal happened then and since, but suffice it to say that we are greatly blessed that our whole family has been able to appreciate a broader racial and cultural world. And it goes without saying that Matt has become the most culturally and racially sensitive of all of our children.

Let me share another example from that same period. We were so busy during those years. We were living in the mission field, and sometimes that requires more service than usual. I was called to be Relief Society president and at the same time the Sunday School chorister and Laurel adviser. I was worried that these demands were robbing me of close mother/child nurturing with my infant daughter, and for years afterward I believed that every colic or croup in her life somehow stemmed from that period of time. My guilt, real or imagined, was immense. But with time and perspective, I can see now that because of my concerns, I probably worked overtime to compensate for my lack of time. This daughter has now turned into a child with great self-confidence. She is very much at home with herself and with me, and ours is one of the most rewarding mother/daughter relationships I know of.

Our family now faces another very demanding challenge. The role of a university president's life can be a full-time job with a generous amount of overtime. With our home situated on the campus, my children won't have friends living next door, and they will have students pointing them out, nicely, but still conspicuously, reminding them that they are the president's children. In a great many ways the years ahead are going to be very difficult and demanding, but they will carry with them their own special blessings and opportunities too, and I intend to make this a very rich and a very rewarding experience. So it seems to me that Shaw is right. You don't simply yield to circumstances. You shape and use them for your own best purposes. Circumstances are seldom ideal, but our ideals can prevail, especially where they affect home and children.

Of the atmosphere surrounding his childhood, President Spencer W. Kimball wrote: "My own wonderful mother's journal records a lifetime of being grateful for the opportunity to serve, and of feeling regretful only that she couldn't do more. I smiled when I recently read one entry, dated January 16, 1900. She was serving as first counselor in the Relief Society presidency in Thatcher, Arizona, and the presidency went to a sister's home where caring for a sick baby had kept the mother from doing her sewing. Mother took her own sewing machine, a picnic lunch, her baby, and a high chair, and they began work. She wrote that night that they had 'made four aprons, four pairs of pants and started a shirt for one of the boys.' They had to stop at four o'clock to go to a funeral, so they did not get any more than that done. I would have been impressed with such an achievement, rather than thinking, 'Well, that's not much.'" President Kimball then went on to say, "That's the kind of home into which I was born, one conducted by a woman who breathed service in all her actions." (*Woman,* Deseret Book, 1979, pp. 1-2.)

Did you know that President Kimball's mother died when he was only eleven when his father was serving as president over a horse-and-buggy stake that stretched from St. Johns to El Paso? Did you know that President McKay was only eight years old when he became the man of the house? His father was called on a mission to Great Britain, two older sisters had just recently died, and his mother was expecting another baby. President McKay's father felt he simply could not leave under those circumstances, but his wife said unequivocally that he would go, adding, "Little David and I will manage this household quite nicely." Did you know that Joseph Fielding Smith was born while his father was serving as a member of the Quorum of the Twelve? He was only four years old when his father became a member of the First Presidency. So sisters, if your husbands are called into the bishopric for a few years, perhaps your children will survive the ordeal quite well. The wonderful thing about these Saints is that they were human.

President Heber J. Grant's father died when Heber was only eight days old. His bishop didn't think young Heber would ever amount to anything because he played baseball too much, but his mother knew what only mothers know, and she molded the future of a young prophet. Did you know that Brigham Young spent his very early years helping his father clear timber off new land and cultivate the ground? He remembered logging and driving teams summer and winter, half clad and with insufficient food until his "stomach would ache." When he was fourteen years old his mother died, leaving the numerous domestic responsibilities to the father and the children.

Do you remember that President Joseph F. Smith was born during those terrible Missouri persecutions? When that little boy was only five years old, he stood over the coffins of his cruelly murdered father and uncle, the Prophet Joseph Smith, as they lay in state in the Nauvoo Mansion House. You know the incredible hardships he and his mother faced as they fought their way west, but what you may not remember is that soon after arriving in Utah, Mary Fielding Smith died, leaving young Joseph an orphan. However, she had done what no one else could do. Her son would later write of her, "Oh my God, how I love and cherish true motherhood! Nothing beneath the celestial kingdom can surpass my deathless love for the sweet, true, noble soul who gave me my birth—my own, own mother! She was good! She was pure! She was indeed a Saint! A royal daughter of God. To her I owe my very existence as also my success in life." (Don Cecil Corbett, *Mary Fielding Smith, Daughter of Britain,* Deseret Book, 1966, p. 268.)

Sisters, when we feel the desire to murmur, when we ask for more means, or more time, or more psychology, or more energy, or even when we wish we just didn't have to do it alone, let's pause and ask one more time, "Is any thing too hard for the Lord?" If a daughter misses one segment in ballet training, perhaps the sun will still shine tomorrow. Had Mary Fielding Smith overheard our contemporary complaints while administering to her stricken ox and raising it from the dead, she might have smiled just a little at our dismay over such things as the price of gasoline. If we seem to lack something found in the homes of our prophets, maybe what we've suffered is not too much affliction but too little. Could it be that the answers are only to be found on our knees as our prophets were required to do while waiting patiently on the Lord?

Now I know that we don't live in the same world with the same challenges our grandmothers or great-grandmothers faced. As the world changes, our challenges seem to be newer and more complex, if not necessarily more heartrending. However, I am convinced that we will fail in our responsibilities if we don't exert the same kind of faith they had. An early-morning run might help us face a laundry crisis, but Christian commandments are necessary for real salvation, both emotional and eternal. Our prayers, for one thing, have to be more earnest and longing, as were our ancestral mothers', if we are to obtain the salvation for which we seek.

Now perhaps you are saying, "But I am praying now; I am faithfully on my knees, and the answers still don't come." All I can say is that the Lord's counsel seems to be to ask more often, however faithfully you are now praying. Are our hands blotchy, as President Kimball said, from knocking at heaven's door? Do we labor in the spirit in any sense that is really labor? I think we, as women, can appreciate that word *labor* in a way that no man ever can. Do we labor spiritually to deliver our children from evil to the degree that we labored to bring them into the world? Is that fair to ask? But is it faithful not to ask? Alma labored much in the spirit, wrestling with God in mighty prayer in an attempt to convince Him to pour out His spirit upon the people. We must do at least as much to call down the spirit into our homes and into the lives of our children. Indeed, this very son, Alma, is a living example of a child who was not only brought to repentance of his former sins but who was also raised up to become one of the Nephites' greatest prophets. All of this was the result of the faith and prayers of a righteous father. When the angel appeared to Alma the younger and the sons of Mosiah, he said, "The Lord hath heard the prayers of his people, and also the prayers of his servant, Alma, who is thy father; for he has prayed with much faith concerning thee; . . . therefore, for this purpose have I come to convince thee of the power and authority of God, that the prayers of his servants might be answered according to their faith." (Mosiah 27:14.)

I believe with all my heart that the prayer of faith is heard, is efficacious, and is answered. I especially believe that to be true when we are praying for others and never more true than when we are praying for our family and children.

Faithful scripture study seems to be another oft-cited yet overlooked habit, but I have personally taken very great comfort from this passing comment from President Kimball, who said of his beloved Camilla, "I think of the spirit of revelation that my own dear wife invites into our home because of the hours she spent every year of our married life in studying the scriptures, so that she can be prepared to teach the principles of the gospel." (*Woman,* p. 1.)

Where should we turn when we hear so many confusing voices trying to define our role as mothers in today's world? Are we studying the illuminating truths of the past, the words for which prophets have died and angels have flown? Can we disregard them—a rich resource of God's clearest instructions to us—and still cry that he has left us alone in a wicked and worrisome world? We should be in the scriptures, as was ancient Israel, both day and night, and then our problems and perplexities will be aided by the spirit of revelation. And so, with simple, traditional, tried and true principles such as earnest prayer, serious scripture study, devoted fasting, compassionate service, and patient forbearance, the blessings of heaven distill upon us even to include the personal manifestation of the Son of God himself. May I close with these two thoughts. The first is from President Harold B. Lee, who said, "If we will live worthy, then the Lord will guide us—by personal appearance, or by His actual voice, or by His voice coming into our mind, or by impressions upon our heart and our soul." (*Stand Ye in Holy Places,* Deseret Book, 1974, p. 144.) And President McKay said, "Pure hearts in a pure home are always in whispering distance of heaven." (Dean Zimmerman, comp., *Sentence Sermons,* Deseret Book, 1978, p. 91.)

I was raised in a pure home by people with pure hearts, and for me that has made all the difference. When my mother was carrying me, my family lived in a tent while my father sought work during the war. Shortly after I was conceived, my mother became very ill and threatened to miscarry. The doctor, whose office was sixty miles away, told her if she were to keep the baby, she would have to go to bed and stay there the entire nine months. She, without complaining, tells of the hardship of trying to keep small, active boys entertained in a tent, which was extremely hot in the summer and cold in the winter, while she lay flat on her back in bed. All of her friends and neighbors counseled her to get up and lose the baby naturally because it would probably be deformed anyway. But my mother lives within whispering distance of heaven, and in a pure heart. In answer to prayer, she had her own private inspiration that let her know that she could and would carry this child. She taught me about prayer, personal sacrifice, endurance, and deep faith. I thank her for her devotion to and reverence for life. Much of what I feel about motherhood and family I inherited from this saintly woman, and in more than the clichéd, standard way, I acknowledge that I owe my life to her.

May I leave my humble testimony that there are answers to all of our anxieties. Some of them may come painfully and some of them may come very, very slowly, but I believe with all my heart they will come if we believe and follow our Lord Jesus Christ.

Patricia T. Holland studied at Dixie College and at Brigham Young University, where her husband, Jeffrey R. Holland, serves as president. Sister Holland is a counselor in the Church's Young Women general presidency.

Responsible Assertiveness: How to Get Along without Giving Up or Getting Out

SALLY H. BARLOW

TAMARA M. QUICK

he word *assertiveness* has a negative connotation for some people. It is often associated with radical movements in America that have earned unfortunate reputations for selfish or "me first" attitudes. However, assertive behavior and the underlying research have been with us through centuries, though under different names: displaying righteous indignation, sticking up for oneself, expressing valid opinions. These phrases connote a much different mental image than do the phrases "letting it all hang out," or "telling it like it is"—regardless of who is hurt or how inappropriately timed the remarks.

Specifically, the assertiveness training technique is based on the assumption that anxiety in social situations is a learned response that can be unlearned and replaced by an assertive response. This becomes a counter-condition to the original anxiety. Successful assertive training has been used with couples, psychiatric patients, shy college males, and passive women. This is only a small sampling of the range of possibilities.

Assertive training is akin to learning any new skill: playing the piano, mastering new math, or pitching a fast ball. All new skills require practice. The more you practice, the better you become, the less awkward you feel employing the new skill, and the broader your communication with others becomes. These elements of learning and improving are important because many people think some are simply born better communicators than others. Although certain variables in genetic imprinting and environmental training do influence the level of skill you emerge with in adulthood, you can always improve any skill. And communication is a skill, not a magic, mystically endowed commodity some have and others don't.

What exactly is assertiveness, and how does it compare with aggressive or passive behavior? Read through the following three examples and select the ones you see as assertive, passive, or aggressive.

1. Dad: Did you get around to mowing the lawn Saturday as I asked you?
   Teen: No, the lawn mower is broken and *you* promised to fix it by then, so it's your fault, not mine. Go pin the blame where it belongs.

2. Dad: Did you get around to mowing the lawn Saturday as I asked you?
   Teen: Well, uh, no. But the mower is kinda broken, and, well, you . . . Never mind, that's ok, I'll do it.

3. Dad: Did you get around to mowing the lawn Saturday as I asked you?
   Teen: Dad, remember you said you'd get the mower fixed, right? I'd do it, but I can't drive yet, and I'm not strong enough to lift the mower in and out of the back of the car by myself. I know you're busy, and I know you really wanted me to have the lawn done. How about if we take it in now, see if we can pick it up tomorrow, and I'll mow the lawn Wednesday evening?

The differences are easy to spot. We didn't vary the father's remarks because that adds another dimension to the exchange. It was the teen's response that took on certain qualities. In the first one, the teen spoke quickly, sharply, and without offering a solution. In the second vignette, the teen backed down without really telling the father what the delay was. One of the things you will notice about the third vignette is that the answer took at least twice as long. Assertive responses usually do, but they are worth the time. Think back to the first situation. The time it will take to wade through what will undoubtedly be an argument will most likely take much longer and will cost more emotional energy than the assertive response. In the second vignette, the teen will probably end up taking much more time simply because the real problem (a broken lawn mower) has not been solved.

Let's look at the elements in the third response. First, the teen openly reminded the father of the original agreement and explained why it couldn't be taken care of without someone else's help. Second, the teen acknowledged how the father might be feeling. Third, the teen suggested a solution to the problem. These are important steps: giving information, empathizing, and suggesting solutions.

While we are aware that most exchanges, even assertive ones, don't go quite that smoothly, it is still important to demonstrate the sequence of steps involved and to convey our belief that with consistent practice, many such exchanges could really sound similar to the assertive one.

Recognizing that we all use parts of the above three styles, we would like to define each style in terms of internal attitudes (intent or point of view), external behaviors (how we look when we behave in certain ways), and the social consequences (how our attitude and behavior affect others and our relationships with them). As you read these descriptions, attempt to identify where you might fit most of the time. For example, do you follow a particular pattern more often than not in potentially uncomfortable situations?

The passive person's attitude is essentially that of avoiding conflict at all cost. Many people grow up believing all conflict is bad. This is unfortunate, because differences create conflict. We have not all been stamped out of the same mold. Yes, we share similarities, but our differences can be delightful if we can muster the courage to express them and work them out through compromise. The person who intends to avoid conflict at all cost ends up behaving in passive ways, giving in, getting walked on, allowing stress to infringe on his or her interpersonal rights. As a consequence, a passive person may feel hurt, anxious, angry on the inside, frustrated, and disrespected. The person who has done the "walking on" may feel guilty, angry, disrespectful, and frustrated as well.

The aggressive person's attitude may be one of dominating or winning at all costs. The behavior displayed is usually direct or indirect attack.[1] The social consequences to the aggressor usually involve an initial sense of power or success, but eventually he or she may end up feeling alienated. It is difficult to maintain relationships that operate in this way. The person who is attacked may feel defensive, humiliated, and manipulated and may even counterattack.

The assertive person's attitude is a hope for honest communication, responsible expression of needs and wants, and an effort to maintain both persons' rights. The behavior usually includes giving information, openly expressing feelings (even the vulnerable ones, such as "I love you" or "I'm angry at you"), and attempting to mutually solve problems or to compromise. The social consequences of such attitudes and behaviors are usually mutual respect and satisfying relationships. It is particularly encouraging to two people in a relationship when they know they can have their occasional differences over ideas, beliefs, and feelings, and still emerge as friends! This consistent care-taking of relationships makes them strong, safe, and sound.

---

[1] A direct attack (open expression of anger) is difficult to take, but it is at least visible, unlike the indirect attack or what is called passive-aggressive. Such an attack occurs without our immediate awareness, although we may register hurt, anger, or disappointment later as the original attack sinks in. The following exchange demonstrates a passive-aggressive remark. (The intent of the indirect attack is to get what the person wants without directly asking for it.)

Susan: Hi, Jane. Your husband certainly looks good when he goes to work. Do you spend all your clothing allowance on him, since you dress plainly—I mean . . . practically?

Jane: (Unsure which part of the remark to respond to) Well, yes, he does look nice, doesn't he.

The theory of learning assertive skills is based on the skill-acquisition model of learning, which involves a number of components: instruction, modeling, role-playing, feedback, reinforcement, and homework. What this boils down to is this:

First, assess where you are now. Keep what is called a "baseline" of your behavior. A good way to do this is to watch yourself during one week and tally on a piece of paper how many times you behaved assertively, passively, or aggressively; what occurred just before your response; and what you would have done differently if you could do it over. This initial assessment will enable you to know what kind of pattern you are in and if a particular kind of conflict or interaction tends to elicit aggressiveness rather than assertiveness. For example, you may find yourself behaving in a consistently aggressive manner with salespeople. But you may find yourself acting passively toward best friends who make demands you think you simply cannot refuse, regardless of the circumstances.

Second, watch other people. Notice how they respond. Do this vicariously by standing aside and watching other people interact. This distance from the emotional content of the situation will give you time to think about what is really going on.

Third, ask for feedback from one or two people you trust. This will help you learn what your behavior looks like from the outside. We do not always have at our disposal Don Quixote's Knight of Mirrors to reflect back to us how we look. Assertively ask your friends to follow these guidelines when giving you feedback: Be descriptive, not evaluative ("I heard your voice get louder when you spoke to your roommate" rather than "You just stood there and yelled at the top of your lungs and looked like a fool"). Be as specific as possible, not general ("When you backed into the pole you went red in the face" rather than "You can't drive very well!"). Deal with the present, not with the accumulated past ("Today you seem mad at me because you aren't talking" rather than "Remember last year when you clammed up and stomped around?"). Be sensitive to timing. Don't give feedback when the person is not ready to hear it. Wait for the appropriate time. Be helpful, not punishing. Base your motives on help, not hurt. Be careful to focus your feedback on behavior that is *possible* to change ("Because you are short, I always have to clip the tops of the bushes. Could we negotiate that? I could get you a ladder," rather than "Why aren't you taller!").

Fourth, practice. Remember when you pretended as a child? Do the same now. Practice assertive responses with a willing partner or even in front of the mirror alone. Anticipate potentially volatile situations and work through several dry runs.

Fifth, keep a diary of your new skill, not only to note successes (which are great as reinforcers) but also to keep track of certain areas of interpersonal relations that may be more difficult than others to deal with.

Sixth, categorize the problem areas. Do they fall into one or several of the following: making requests, refusing requests, giving compliments, receiving compliments, giving constructive criticism, coping with criticism given to you? Determine the areas in which you are most likely to behave assertively and which will take more practice.

Once you have worked on these ideas and practiced them, several thoughts may occur. One might be, "I realize this is hard work and I should keep trying, but is there ever a time when I should give up?" Yes. There are times when some people in certain situations do not intend ever to let you be able to be yourself or to exercise your integrity or personal rights. Though this is a difficult outcome to admit, it is sometimes better to remove yourself from the relationship, or at least from those interactions that consistently do harm to you. One way to judge this is to assess if, after repeated interactions, you consistently walk away feeling bad. Perhaps the best image that describes such a feeling is "having the wind knocked out of your sails." For whatever reason, the other person has some need to take away things that are meaningful to you, as the following example illustrates:

Ann: I just received an award that I've been working very hard for!

Laura: Oh? That award only took me a week to earn.

These situations can range all the way from critically meaningful to your core personality (moral values) to benignly meaningful, but *still* meaningful, to your sense of self (style of clothes).

Another thought that might occur to you as you practice these skills is the following: "Are there times when I could be responsibly assertive and still feel as if I'm getting nowhere?" Though less severe than the first thought of losing a relationship, it is still disconcerting to find out that some people simply will not change even when treated with respect and honesty. This does not mean you have to end the friendship; rather, it probably means the other person is vulnerable and hence highly defensive in certain areas (that person never listens or responds when you try to negotiate money matters, political issues, or relationship disputes). Once you have tried, the best you can do is accept the situation and, more importantly, acknowledge to yourself that you *still* have integrity for behaving in a responsible and honest way. By resorting to passivity in this kind of situation, you only demean yourself.

A third thought that might strike you while practicing these skills is, "What happens when I am really angry? I don't feel able to think clearly. How can I employ assertive skills that require at least some cognition?" We do feel anger from time to time. It is usually debilitating in the sense that we temporarily lose control of our cognitive capabilities. You can do several things: stay in the arena and see what happens, leave until you feel in control, or acknowledge how mad you feel and set up a time to talk later. (That way, the other person knows you are interested enough in him or her to actually "make an appointment" to clear the air, and that you simply want to leave before you do something both of you might regret. Remember, any argument can be pursued at a later time, when you are better able to use assertive skills.)

These exceptions to the rule are part and parcel of learning a new skill, experiencing doubts about its efficacy, and incorporating the skill as a viable part of our response repertoire.

The skills associated with the interactive styles discussed here might appropriately be called "Christian behavior" or "responsible Christianity." The Savior gave us the model for our behavior in relationships. His teachings, both by precept and by example, give guidelines for our conduct. These teachings address the struggles involved in improving the quality of our interactions. The focus of such teaching is not just on *attitudes* of brotherly love, but also on *actions*—actual behaviors of brotherly love in everyday life.

These skills outline some specific methods of relating to our brothers and sisters within this Christian framework. The counsel given to us in Doctrine and Covenants 121:41-46 discusses methods for successful relationships. Assertive behavior involves just such an authentic and pervasive attitude of brotherly love ("kindness," "without hypocrisy . . . guile," "love unfeigned") coupled with willingness to confront inappropriate behavior ("reproving betimes with sharpness") in order to improve the quality of relationships.

Christian living is not simple. Much of the pain and distress we encounter daily seems to inveigh against the practice of Christian living. The methods and skills we have discussed are grounded not just in sound psychological theories and practices but ultimately in the principles of relationship-building taught and practiced by the Savior and his disciples before and after the meridian of time. The Savior acknowledged and taught the concept of progression toward perfection rather than overnight transformation. He offered hope to overcome our frailties.

The challenge in practicing assertive behavior is to first develop the desire to respond lovingly in our relationships. Then the employment of the skills and techniques will expand beyond mere techniques or "trickery," which seem contrived, into genuine feelings of caring, which are real.

The cautions are obvious. Technique without heart is worse than bumbling ineptness. Relationships of value require, as the scripture admonishes, "love unfeigned." Sensational transformations are neither possible nor very believable; rather, steady progress is more feasible. The rewards of responsible assertiveness will be the result. Over a period of time more satisfying and appropriately intimate relationships, which are essential to our mental health and spiritual growth, will develop.

References

Alberti, R. E., & Emmons, M. L., *Your Perfect Right: A Guide to Assertive Behavior.* San Luis Obispo, California: Impact, 1970, 1974.

Barlow, S. H. "Responsible Assertiveness for Couples," in M. Hoopes, B. Fisher, S. Barlow, *Family Facilitation Programs.* Maryland: Aspen Systems Corp.

Carkhuff, R. *Helping and Human Relations* (vols. 1 & 2). New York: Holt, Rinehart and Winston, 1969.

Fensterheim, H., & Baer, J. *Don't Say Yes When You Want to Say No.* New York: Dell Publishing, 1975.

Gutride, M., Goldstein, A., & Hunter, G. F. "The Use of Modeling and Role Playing to Increase Social Interaction Among Asocial Psychiatric Patients." *Journal of Consulting and Clinical Psychology* 40 (1973): 408-15.

Jakubowski-Spector, P. "Facilitating the Growth of Women Through Assertive Training." *The Counseling Psychologist* 4 (1973): 75-87.

Mace, D., & Mace, V. "The Selection, Training, and Certification of Facilitators for Marriage Enrichment Programs." *The Family Coordinator,* April 1976, pp. 117-25.

Mandarino, M. University of Utah College of Nursing. Telephone conversation regarding "Ideas to Keep in Mind" handouts. Fall, 1976.

McFall, R., & Marsten, A. "An Experimental Investigation of Behavioral Rehearsal in Assertive Training." *Journal of Abnormal Psychology* 76 (1970): 293-303.

Russell, R. A. "Assertiveness Training and Its Effects upon the Marital Relationship." *Family Therapy* 8 (1981): 19-20.

Smith, M. J. *When I Say No, I Feel Guilty.* New York: Dial Press, 1975.

Twentymen, C. T., & McFall, R. M. "Behavioral Training of Social Skills in Shy Males." *Journal of Consulting and Clinical Psychology* 43 (1975), 384-95.

Wolpe, J. *The Practice of Behavior Therapy.* New York: Pergamon Press, 1969.

Wolpe, J., & Lazarus, A. *Behavior Therapy Techniques.* New York: Pergamon Press, 1966.

Sally H. Barlow is associate professor of psychology at Brigham Young University. She received her training at the University of Utah, where she interned in the counseling center and was an academic advisement counselor. Tamara M. Quick, director of student programs at BYU, received her academic training at BYU and at Teachers College, Columbia University.

Scholars of the Scriptures

MAREN M. MOURITSEN

y father was my scriptural mentor. I don't recall that he read very many books—perhaps the Church magazines. He wasn't a scholar in that sense. But he understood gospel principles and knew the scriptures better than any other person I have known. And he instilled that same love of the gospel in all his children. It is my blessing to have acquired his love for the scriptures.

The only grandparent I knew was my maternal grandmother. On my eighth birthday—after her death—my father gave me her large, gold-embossed, well-used family Bible. Today it rests in the living room of my home. When I turned twelve, my father and I rode ponies into the Arizona desert. We sat beneath mesquite trees and talked of the importance of becoming twelve years of age, not only because that is when a young man accepts the responsibility of the priesthood, but also because it is when a young woman accepts responsibility in the gospel. At that time he gave me his most prized possession, a 1912 Liverpool edition of the Book of Mormon, Doctrine and Commandments, and Pearl of Great Price. These scriptures have gone on three missions—my grandfather's, my father's, and my own mission to Japan—and they are among my most revered possessions. The scriptures, then, have always been an important part of our family.

A story is told of a gifted musician who could identify with total accuracy each of any ten notes played simultaneously on a piano. When an admirer asked how he did it, he answered, "They are my friends." I have reflected on this story many times in the context of the gospel. As I leaf through my scriptures, they sometimes fall open to a verse I have read often, that I have anguished over. I love them because they are my friends.

And they can become your friends too—but not without a struggle. The Lord said, "It shall come to pass, that if you are faithful you shall receive the fulness of the record of John. I give unto you these sayings that you may understand and know how to worship, and know what you worship, that you may come unto the Father in my name, and in due time receive of his fulness." (D&C 93:18-19.) I have a little volume entitled *The Gospel According to Peanuts.* In one of the cartoons, Charlie Brown and Lucy are leaning on a fence and Lucy is saying, "My father has been reading a lot lately. He's studying theology, history, communications, and political science." Charlie Brown responds, "Has it helped him?" And Lucy says, "Oh, yes. It takes his mind off his bowling." Compare that with Parley P. Pratt's first reading of the Book of Mormon: "I couldn't eat. I couldn't sleep. I just wanted to read the book." It is not simply a matter of taking our minds off bowling; it is a matter of becoming what I call "intellectually intoxicated"—intoxicated on the fruits of inquiry, insight, and inspiration.

Today I would like to explore five issues related to the achievement of that intoxication.

1. *How Do We Become Scholars?*

The scriptures are decisive when they state, "The glory of God is intelligence, or, in other words, light and truth." (D&C 93:36.) To obtain his glory and become like him is our commission. To achieve that end, we must testify and act according to our knowledge of the truth. In a theological context that seems logical, but there is a catch: "Behold, here is the agency of man, and here is the condemnation of man; because that which from the beginning is plainly manifest unto them, and they receive not the light. . . . And that wicked one cometh and taketh away light and truth, through disobedience, from the children of men, and because of the tradition of their fathers." (D&C 93:31, 39.) If it is because we *will* not receive the light that we lose access to the truth, it seems imperative that we determine how to obtain the light.

But what is the process? How do we distinguish the immature arrogance of dogma from the enlightened principles that testify of light and truth? The *quest* is to live our lives in a world that "lieth in sin, and groaneth under darkness" (D&C 84:49) and to "live by every word that proceedeth forth from the mouth of God" (D&C 84:44). The *challenge* is to know the difference.

Inquiry. How do we get truth? How did the boy prophet, Joseph Smith, do it? First he searched the scriptures. And what did they tell him to do? "Ask of God." (See James 1:5.) The initial step is the question, the inquiry. Truth and the gospel will answer any question you wish to pose—which is not to say that you will get an immediate answer or that you will always be entirely satisfied. When we desire light and knowledge, we must first ask, not belligerently or doubtfully, but in a spirit of genuine inquiry. "Which church is right?" Each of us must at some time ask that question and receive our own personal answer.

Insight. The next step in obtaining a knowledge of the truth is to acquire insight. Understanding. A fresh perspective. Addressing the manner in which we can discern good from evil, Mormon provided us with a good definition of insight: "The way to judge is as plain, that ye may know with a perfect knowledge, as the daylight is from the dark of night. For behold, the Spirit of Christ is given to every man. . . . And now, my brethren, seeing that ye know the light by which ye may judge, which light is the light of Christ, see that ye do not judge wrongfully." (Moroni 7:15-16, 18.) This critical link, insight, is given to every human being. It is, indeed, the light of Christ, which makes possible the genius of the world as manifest in the works of our great scientists, thinkers, artists, humanitarians, and others. It is that exceptional ability to formulate ideas and to generate flashes of brilliance that brings masterpieces into the world. But while it is significant, insight is not the ultimate source of light. What, then, is missing? The third critical component: inspiration.

Inspiration. In its ultimate form, inspiration comes, not temporarily but permanently, as an added confirmation or personal revelation. (See D&C 8:2-3.) Its source is the Holy Ghost, who knows all things. Through the laying on of hands, and predicated upon continued worthiness, one's life is permeated with the influence of the Holy Ghost. Experientially as well as spiritually, we are caught in the spirit of revelation. Conceived in commitment, nurtured in consecration of self, and matured in the bending of every knee, the ultimate manifestation is testimony. But once we have a testimony, we just start all over again. We don't say, "Well, now I've got a testimony, I'm home free. I can quit." No, we get a testimony of one thing and then of another. And pretty soon we have a testimony of the gospel of Jesus Christ—that he lives, that he is our Redeemer, that life is eternal, that we can become like him.

Faith. In the Doctrine and Covenants, the Lord speaks to Oliver Cowdery regarding the translation of the gold plates. "Assuredly as the Lord liveth, who is your God and your Redeemer, even so surely shall you receive a knowledge of whatsoever things you shall ask in faith, with an honest heart, believing that you shall receive a knowledge concerning the engravings of old records." (D&C 8:1.) The key is an honest heart that asks in faith.

Alma 32 talks about the importance of putting the Lord's word to the test by planting the seed, which will germinate only if there is the element of faith. This element is the common denominator in the process of obtaining truth. During the drug era, when those involved talked about mind expansion, it always struck me that they didn't really understand the process. They had to do it through artificial inducement. There is a way, however, through which one can become excited, exhilarated, and expanded in a righteous context. One of the marvelous things about Alma 32:34 is the part that says, "Yea, your knowledge is perfect in that thing, and your faith is dormant."

There comes a point when we have such an assurance, such pure knowledge, and such an implanting of pure truth, that we no longer need faith on that issue. Through this process, pure knowledge and ultimate truth somehow become bonded into testimony. At that point, we can apply that measure of faith toward the discovery of something else. We can begin to experiment upon another seed.

We read further, and Alma talks about laying aside our faith when we have pure knowledge but continuing to plant seeds and to grow. And then, in Alma 34:42, we read, "Because of your diligence and your faith and your patience with the word in nourishing it, that it may take root in you, behold, by and by ye shall pluck the fruit thereof."

Now, what happens after we have asked the question and have had some insight, some inspiration, and some faith?

Trial and agency. Even after all this, we do not always receive an answer; instead we often receive a trial of our faith. (See D&C 105:19.) Then comes the real task—choosing. Using our agency, we must choose good from evil, right from wrong, light from darkness, a burning in the bosom from a stupor of thought, for this is the Savior's way.

2. What Is the Meaning of Our Struggle?

For many years I have been struck not only by the sheer energy of our ancestors, but also by their incredible strength. They were not, as some have suggested, illiterate or unskilled. There were marvelous craftsmen and brilliant scholars among them. They asked probing questions and wrote marvelously about the nature of God and Christ and of our relationship to them. Beginning with the boy prophet, they were willing to pay the price.

Our test is not to cross mountains on bloody feet or to bear and even bury our young on dusty plains. Those were the Aaronic tests—the outward ordinances. Today we are confronting the Melchizedek tests. We are dealing with matters of the mind in a way that we have never dealt with them before. But do we stop long enough to ask questions and labor for answers? Or are we too busy substituting frantic activity as we seek to become Molly or Master Mormon? Despite the completeness of our theology, we are still struggling to find the motivation and the modus operandi for applying gospel principles in our daily lives.

We moderns have lost a lot of our agency. Often we elect to be acted upon rather than to act. When we become so frantically involved that we cease to look within and be touched by the Spirit, we are in the employ of the devil; we become his chattel. It takes a great effort to recover from that condition. In addition, we have given up some of our individuality—an individuality that is stressed so often in the gospel and the scriptures. Nephi and Alma, for example, understood the importance of individualizing learning. Alma said:

> It is given unto many to know the mysteries of God; nevertheless they are laid under a strict command that they shall not impart only according to the portion of his word which he doth grant unto the children of men, according to the heed and diligence which they give unto him.
>
> And therefore, he that will harden his heart, the same receiveth the lesser portion of the word; and he that will not harden his heart, to him is given the greater portion of the word, until it is given unto him to know the mysteries of God until he knoweth them in full.
>
> And they that will harden their hearts, to them is given the lesser portion of the word until they know nothing concerning his mysteries; and then they are taken captive by the devil, and led by his will down to destruction. Now this is what is meant by the chains of hell. (Alma 12:9-11.)

Through these three verses we learn what it means to be chained—a chaining that comes when we lose knowledge, when we give up our quest for knowledge. The Savior's teachings also take into account individual needs: "Blessed are those who hearken unto my precepts, and lend an ear unto my counsel, for they shall learn wisdom; for unto him that receiveth I will give more; and from them that shall say, We have enough, from them shall be taken away even that which they have." (2 Nephi 28:30.) In other words, he will take us by the hand and support us if we are committed to doing what he says. Pray, fast, study, and work. Devote the time.

Knowledge is given in increments to each searcher, and the key to the retention of that knowledge is found in how we obtain it, why we obtain it, and how we apply it in our lives. Thus, we are involved in an enormous struggle to know his way and do his will, yet to be ourselves.

3. *Why Are the Scriptures Valuable?*

How do I apply the scriptures to my life? From a myriad of reasons, I have isolated six:

First, the scriptures are weighted to persuade men to believe in the Lord and to keep his commandments, that we might humble ourselves and in so doing become truly converted. What a mighty exercise! Nephi and Mosiah talk about their struggles to understand and teach the words of God so that an entire generation might not suffer in ignorance. (See 1 Nephi 19:23; Mosiah 1:2-7.)

Second, the scriptures reveal the gospel of Jesus Christ. Alma states that all things come of God and are laid before us in the scriptures. (See Alma 30:44.) And in the Doctrine and Covenants, the Lord declares plainly and simply that we have the Bible and the Book of Mormon, which together contain the fullness of the gospel. (See D&C 42:12.)

Third, the scriptures teach us to follow the prophets' examples. It is not necessary to experience sin in life to know what sin is. Nephi declares, "And now, whoso readeth, let him understand; he that hath the scriptures, let him search them, and see and behold if all these deaths and destructions by fire, and by smoke, and by tempests, and by whirlwinds, and by the opening of the earth to receive them, and all these things are not unto the fulfilling of the prophecies of many of the holy prophets." (3 Nephi 10:14.)

Fourth, the scriptures teach us the law. In a brief discourse, Nehemiah makes this point clearly and succinctly: "So they [the Levites] read in the book in the law of God distinctly, and gave the sense, and caused them [the children of Israel] to understand the reading." (Nehemiah 8:8.) There are eternal laws that govern us. It is imperative that we know and understand these laws if we are to abide God's light as well as in his kingdom.

Fifth, the scriptures teach us those things that we should be doing in our lives. We will be judged out of those books; it is incumbent upon us to know the contents of those books. "Angels speak by the power of the Holy Ghost; wherefore, they speak the words of Christ. Wherefore, I said unto you, feast upon the words of Christ; for behold, the words of Christ will tell you all things what ye should do." (2 Nephi 32:3.) The steps are seldom specified; that is, we will not often read a scripture specifying that if we follow steps one, two, and three we will gain salvation—or four, five, six to exaltation. But somewhere, and everywhere, between the covers of these books are all the things we need to understand, all the things we need to know, all the things we need to be and do in order to gain exaltation and eternal life. It is imperative that each of us search and find our own individual path.

Sixth, the scriptures help us know God. Nephi told us that if we haven't read the scriptures and don't know God's name, we cannot expect to be counted among his saints in the latter days. (See 3 Nephi 27:5.) We must know the scriptures to be able to know him. We must understand the restoration of the gospel if we are to become his disciples. (See also Jeremiah 9:23-24; 2 Nephi 19:23.)

Section 84 of the Doctrine and Covenants relates well to this concept of discipleship. In addition to talking about the oath and covenant of the priesthood, it discusses the power of discipleship (which, incidentally, has nothing to do with maleness or femaleness). The power of being a disciple and the importance of being an example to the world are at the core of this section. On the other hand, in three short verses, section 40 sets forth the sad story of James Covill—his blessing and his spiritual obituary. It is a poignant example of lost discipleship.

The scriptures are valuable to me because they are my measure of truth. I am a better person when I read them daily and am engaged in an honest effort to implement them in my life.

4. *What Is the Promise of the Scriptures?*

This discussion will be brief because the promise is very specific. The challenge is to be perfect. (See 3 Nephi 12:48.) But the promise is that we can meet the challenge and thereby gain eternal life: "Wherefore, ye must press forward with a steadfastness in Christ, having a perfect brightness of hope, and a love of God and of all men [the first and second great commandments: Love God and fellowman]. Wherefore, if ye shall press forward, feasting upon the word of Christ, and endure to the end, behold, thus saith the Father: Ye shall have eternal life." (2 Nephi 31:20.)

My responsibility is to find my own pathway back home. In the struggle, I welcome the assurance from my Savior that I can find the path. And I acknowledge my responsibility to help my brothers and sisters who are also seeking.

5. *What Are Some Practical Tools for Studying the Scriptures?*

Let us conclude by talking about "How to's." Although my methods might not be yours, I am sharing mine because I always enjoy hearing others'.

Mosiah and Alma speak about some attributes that prepare us for scriptural study. Mosiah states plainly that we should not "trifle" but be serious and open our ears that our hearts may understand. (See Mosiah 2:9.) Are we attentive in meetings? Do we discuss the principles of the gospel with others? Probably we can do better.

In describing the sons of Mosiah, Alma used some very specific characteristics: "Now these sons of Mosiah were with Alma at the time the angel first appeared unto him; . . . yea, and they had waxed strong in the knowledge of truth; for they were men of sound understanding and they had *searched the scriptures diligently. . . .* But this is not all; they had given themselves to much *prayer, and fasting;* therefore they had the spirit of prophecy, and the spirit of revelation, and when they taught, they taught with power and authority of God." (Alma 17:2-3; italics added.) We too must search with diligence through prayer and fasting. These are vital principles that must be taken seriously and applied with diligence.

I love to draw, and I tend not only to see but also to remember things best through the use of visual motifs. Therefore, when I study I draw charts, maps, lists, and so on. For example, there was a time when I became intensely interested in the twelve tribes of Israel. I felt that I could not possibly understand my personal destiny unless I understood the twelve tribes, and I devoted two years to learning all that I could about them.

I started by taking Bruce R. McConkie's *Mormon Doctrine* (there are a number of topical books from which to select) and reading every reference and checking every source relating to the twelve tribes. As I read, I carefully documented all of my questions, concerns, and interests. I then went to the concordance of each of the standard works until I had looked up every possible reference. After I had read virtually thousands of related scriptures, I began to focus on relationships and patterns. I bought inexpensive editions of the scriptures and cut them up, putting them side by side and even pasting them on mirrors and cupboards in order to become more familiar with how the scriptures either varied or were complementary.

At this point, I started to make lists and charts (my folder on this topic is some five inches thick). I first began a chart of the genealogy of the twelve tribes on an 8½-by-11-inch sheet of paper, only to discover that the Lord had many things to say specifically about Abraham as he relates to the twelve tribes. So I started a page for Abraham; then I started one for Jacob; then I started one for Isaac. Soon I had a myriad of sheets. As I was correlating all these scriptures and sheets, significant patterns began to emerge. Suddenly stories that were once only tales took on glorious historical as well as theological import. So complex was my involvement that my 8½-by-11-inch sheets became inadequate to handle the increasingly complex relationships. Undaunted, I took out a bed sheet and tacked it to my study wall, bought a box of colored marking pens, and began one of the most incredible adventures I have ever experienced.

I worked on that sheet for more than a year. It became as re-vered as any medieval tapestry.

Pretty soon I understood why the birthright had to be Jacob's rather than Esau's, what was important about the re-lationship between Solomon and David, why the Savior had to come through the house of David, why it was Moroni who had to appear to Joseph Smith, and more. It was all there. It was sys-tematic and orderly. The Lord did have a plan. He knew exactly what he was doing. For the first time, I, Maren Mouritsen, un-derstood my own destiny and what it meant to be a Latter-day Saint. I was elect; I was blessed. For the first time I understood clearly the covenants with the House of Israel, and the purpose behind the endowment.

My project took me almost two years and no less than thirty minutes every day. That's one approach. Instead of saying, "I think I'll start at the front of the New Testament and just read through it," take a topic and probe it in depth. Play all its keys. Become friends. There are many things I never saw in the scrip-tures until I began looking at them topically and specifically. In addition, I try to listen to a tape recording of my daily scriptural reading. This enables me to detect nuances that I would miss if I only read *or* listen. I also seek out those people with whom I can discuss the scriptures not only deeply but also openly. Ex-ploring reasonable avenues is cake; the speculative is the frost-ing. It takes time, but it is well worth it. Currently, I am studying the Fall. It has been my pet project for the past five years.

Once you become intimate friends with the scriptures, you begin to understand much more than is sometimes written. Of course, such projection is speculative and has to be recognized as such, but it can be very exciting, rather like a whodunit. An example: Who was Tabitha? Many of you know who Tabitha was. She was a character in the New Testament, often called Dorcus. Dorcus was a name given to women who were consid-ered to be of the elect. It means "gazelle," "beautiful," "active," "vital."

Our intrigue begins at Tabitha's death. The women wept and brought clothing that she might be prepared for burial—much as our Relief Society sisters might do today. The disciples in the area had sent two men, possibly missionaries, to summon Peter, the president of the church. Although he was in Joppa, he came immediately. He went to the upper chamber, where Dorcus lay, extended his hand, and commanded that she arise. When she did so, he lifted her up and took her downstairs to be presented to those waiting.

It's an interesting, even a touching story. But as I read the details, some questions come to mind. Some of these insights have been refined in a speculative gospel discussion with one of those dear and trusted friends I mentioned earlier. Why would the president of the church come all the way from Joppa to be at this woman's side? Why did the sisters bring clothing that had been prepared? When Peter extended his hand and Dorcus arose, why were the sisters crying so? When the Prophet Joseph Smith instituted the Relief Society, he said he was turning the key for women, that the Church wasn't complete without the Relief Society. But we know that the Church was complete at the meridian of time. Could it be that the women were organized, that Dorcus was the president of the Relief Society, and that because of her calling, Peter had come to be at the side of this "elect lady"? I don't know, but it's fun to think about it.

The more I study the scriptures, the more questions I have to ponder, the more thinking I must do—and the more desire I have to explore. In terms of my eternal salvation it really doesn't matter if Tabitha, called Dorcus, was or was not president of the Relief Society. As a scholar and a student, however, I find the possibility exciting, because to me learning is delightsome and sweet. If our goal is to become like the Lord, we must have a great urging, a great exhilaration, a great desire to learn of him. Nothing could be more compelling than to lose oneself in the process of giving oneself. When I study, I do just that, for one of the joys of studying is to forget oneself in immortality.

In closing, I would like to share a few lines from Tolkein's *Fellowship of the Ring:*

"'I wish,' said Frodo, 'it need not have happened in my time.'

"'So do I,' replied Gandalf, 'and so do all those who live to see such times. But that is not for them to decide. All we have to decide is what to do with the time that is given us.'" (New York: Ballantine, 1965, p. 82.)

The methods and processes we have considered work. So whatever your gifts, whatever your endowments, whatever your opportunities—indeed, whatever your burdens—now is the time to decide to become scholars of the scriptures lest the children of our mortal minds become the orphans of our immortal souls.

I testify that the gospel of Jesus Christ is true and that to be motivated to study will infuse your being and your very living with knowledge, light, and testimony. In so doing lies the potential to fulfill God's grand purpose of bringing to pass "the immortality and eternal life of man."

Maren M. Mouritsen, assistant vice-president of Brigham Young University, received her bachelor's degree from Northwestern University and her master's and doctoral degrees from Columbia University.

Being Well Balanced:
A Key to Mental Health

LIBBY R. HIRSH, M.D.

resident Spencer W. Kimball declared: "One skill or attribute need not be developed at the expense of another. Symmetry in our spiritual development is much to be desired." (*Ensign,* November 1978, p. 104.) This teaching is of great importance to us because it emphasizes that we cannot grow and develop only one part of ourselves to the exclusion of others; to do so becomes the first step on the road to disappointment, or worse.

Let me begin by reminding you of someone we all know well—or who we think is in our midst (although in reality this may be far from the truth). Our fictitious friend goes by the name of "Patti Perfect," and she was first brought to our attention by two sisters from Orem—Margaret Black and Midge Nelson—in the spring of 1979. (See "Patti Perfect," *Exponent II,* vol. 5 [1979], no. 3.) From Patti's 5:00 A.M. jogging to her midmorning supervision and baking, through her afternoon's work as a special education director, her visits with relatives, her "quality time" with her children, and her projects, to the culminating evening trip to the temple with her husband, Paul Perfect—she overwhelms us with her absolute perfection. We are awed by the success that marks every aspect of her life. But after our moments of awe, some of us begin to think, "This is really sickening!" Nevertheless, having met up with Patti is absolutely wonderful. She is one of those lovely creatures we all really believe we should be, although in actuality none of us is likely to achieve anything even close. In fact, if Patti teaches us anything, it should be that if some persons *are* coming close, they are doing so at tremendous personal cost. These are the women for whom outside faces and at-home realities could never be the same. But the dilemma is that while we tend to laugh at the thought of "Patti Perfect," we often feel we are not doing enough. We feel we must do all things at once but then feel we have no handle on our own lives.

In an enlightening discussion in which I was recently involved, I heard two very good quotations from past Church leaders that beautifully illustrate the kind of dichotomy we sometimes face in the Church. The first is from Heber C. Kimball, who stressed the principle of obedience (which, of course, is very important) by saying, in essence, "Do what you are told; don't be concerned if it's right or not. If it's wrong, it will be upon the heads of the leaders." The parallel quotation is from Brigham Young, who expressed his great concern that people within the Church were going about as mindless robots. He feared that the people were becoming blind, putting too much trust in their leaders, allowing themselves to believe what was fed to them, never really *thinking* about anything. In our own lives, and certainly in Utah, we can relate to Brigham's fear.

My greatest difficulty as a resident of Utah—and surely this must by why the anti-Mormon sentiment is so strong here (as it is *not* in the mission field)—results from my encounters with complacent Mormons. These are people who do not try to put things in perspective or make any sense of what we are asked to understand. Certainly I am not opposed to following the teachings of Church leaders, but how often do we understand those things with surety and receive our own witness? Have we learned to rely truly on our own strengths and not those of others? Doing so is absolutely necessary if we are to live a life characterized by balance.

In addressing the issue of balance and mental health, I

should like to point out those problems that can result when we do not stay in balance, before looking specifically at what can help us to stay in balance. You most likely know the outcomes of imbalance: physical illnesses, "garden variety" anxiety crowding into our days, tension, feeling "uptight," and so on. All of us feel these things to some degree in our day-to-day living. Yet with more stresses, the cycle may lead to more serious physical difficulties, chronic complaints, and depression. Many people whose bodies give them aches and pains would do well to understand that their head is the source of many of these problems. In fact, national statistics indicate that some 80 percent of all persons consulting their family doctor or internist do so for complaints that ultimately turn out to be psychosomatic, which means that for many of us with chronic headaches, backaches, and so on, our only relief may be to resolve the ongoing stresses in our lives and learn to express these things verbally or in action rather than through our bodies.

I would like to discuss for a moment KSL-TV's production "Depression and Mormon Women." I felt privileged to be a part of that effort, and I would like to tell you how the opportunity came to me. The story is particularly pertinent to our discussion of keeping in balance. The documentary was put together by Louise Degn, a very talented producer and writer for the KSL-TV series "Dimension Five." Louise and I had known each other in Chicago, when I was in medical school and she was working for WBBM-TV. We went to the same ward. When Louise moved back to Utah, I lost track of her. Then, some months after my arrival here, I stumbled onto her name, voice, and picture as I watched the evening news. The result was a renewal of acquaintance and then a fortuitous mesh of common concerns.

At that time I was working at the inpatient psychiatric ward of the University of Utah Medical Center, and when Louise asked me if I saw any one problem more frequently than others, I could only respond with an emphatic yes—that our biggest problem was common to Mormon women, many so very young: They felt terribly depressed and, what is worse, terribly guilty about being depressed. Nor did they know how to handle it. Later Louise explained that she was working on a project regarding depression among Mormon women and asked me for sources to speak with.

At that time my knowledge of Salt Lake LDS psychiatrists and counselors was limited, but I gave her several names and great encouragement to go to them. To my surprise, not *one* of them would speak to her even on tape, much less on film. I was quite nonplussed by this, and I began to wonder if there really was a "big brother" I did not know about. So in the original version of the documentary, all the professional sources other than myself were from outside Utah. Amazing—all of a sudden I became an expert! In the expanded version—the one that finally was aired—we were able to get more local people because, after considerable press and promotion, the original film was pulled two days before it was due to be aired. And what a reaction that created! My non-Mormon colleagues at work, who felt it was time that the Church take an honest look at itself and had been glad it was happening, turned to saying, "See, we knew they couldn't do it; they'll never be able to face their problems." But the furor surrounding the cancellation made people aware that something was really up, and many came forward to express their own views or to share their personal experiences.

Perhaps we will never know the full story of why the film was pulled, but one of the stories that circulates is that someone in the Church was offended by a statement made by one psychiatrist who, when asked if Mormon women were any more or less depressed than women in general, said, no, he felt they were "just people." To me, we have a tremendous problem if we are not allowed to consider ourselves "just people." Perhaps we in the Church are lucky, being somewhat "the elect," but every person on this earth is a spirit child of our Heavenly Father.

In any case, the film did air, and the rest is history. Certainly my life and the lives of many of the participants have been changed as a result. And we have seen great changes in many other women's lives. For example, the statistics at community mental health centers and within private practitioners' files all reflect an abrupt jump in the number of people finally getting

the help they need. The personal gratification is truly great. I recall one woman who came to me from Vernal, Utah. She had
been depressed for eight years, had seen perhaps ten different
counselors in that time who for whatever reason had not recognized her difficulty, had nearly killed herself on four different
occasions, and was totally disheartened. She had even thought
of asking her bishop to excommunicate her because she believed that her continued suffering must only reflect her un-
worthiness. Nine months later, this woman was an entirely different person—and this was the result of recognizing and then
treating her depression.

For another person, a young woman my own age, depression had had its onset in her teens, leaving her swinging forever
from day to day as moods would come and go. The negative effects on her self-esteem and the guilt this caused led to devastat-
ing effects. Her well-meaning parents would tell her of her
faults, and she would work diligently to correct them, yet in the
end she never felt any better. Then, after years of suffering, she
arrived at the conclusion that her suffering resulted from some
innate weakness. A disrupted marriage, a turning away from the
standards of the Church, prescribed medication to "take her
away from her pain," and the like—all, she believed, had been
caused by her weaknesses.

This person ultimately elected to pull herself together
again. She remarried in the temple, sacrificed for husband and
children, and did as many things as could be humanly expected
in her striving toward that great pinnacle of—who else?—Patti
Perfect. But she did not feel any better. Having material comforts for the first time in her life had no effect on her. She would
read in the scriptures for hours, fast, pray, and request innumerable blessings. People outside her family would fast and pray
for her. Still she did not recover, and these same people then
led her to believe that she was depressed "of the devil" and that
she was "allowing" this (!) by just giving in. This woman took
countless self-help classes, read the best of books, followed all
the platitudes and prescriptions friends and family would dic-
tate—yet the more she did, the more worthless she felt. She
questioned all of her talents and abilities, and eventually she

reached the incredible conclusion that her place and circumstances must surely reflect her having done so badly in the premortal existence that she would be required to *learn* more things through suffering in this life than perhaps any other soul who has dwelled here.

May I now tell you of the other side of the coin? This woman has been cured of her depression, and she now describes feeling much more spiritually in tune than she had during all those years of weekly temple attendance, fasting, and so on. She describes the Spirit as coming to her only when she is relaxed and feels good about herself. In her constant efforts to draw it into her life before, she experienced only failure and the ultimate realization that it cannot come in such a forced context. So many women (and men) suffer these difficulties! And how much we could enrich their lives and our own if we would learn to recognize vulnerabilities, define problems, and then put this knowledge into practice.

So what about this problem of depression? It is very common. As a matter of fact, as I list many of the symptoms and how depression affects one's life, you may say, "Has she been in my house?" No, I haven't. It is just that these problems are predictable, real, and can confront all of us. Let me give you some statistics to start with, as it is worthwhile for us all to be aware of the magnitude of the problem. The National Institutes of Mental Health estimate that at some point in life, 25 percent of the population will experience a significant depression—not a brief dejection, but something sustained and of sufficient severity to require some form of outside help. What is even more significant is that of all persons who become depressed, at least two-thirds are women. This is not a statistical fluke. Many arguments attempt to explain away this phenomenon, saying women just complain more, women go to doctors more, women are given "soft" diagnoses while men get called things like "passive-aggressive," and women are freer to let others know of their problems and pain. However, a very comprehensive study by Yale University revealed the hard fact that almost three-fourths of all depressions occur in women. There are some things about us, then—perhaps parts of our biology (some aspects we have yet to specifically define), and certainly things about us culturally—that make us, as a group, more prone to depression. Insofar as this is true, we would do well to become aware of the syndrome—its symptoms, what others see, what it comes from, and how we may get help and get better if we should experience it.

Symptoms of Depression

We can group the symptoms of the depressive syndrome (I say syndrome because its specific causes are many) into three major categories. Given these frameworks, it may then be easier for us to comprehend the total picture of depression.

The first category, probably the most familiar, represents all those *feeling* states and attributes that the depressed person experiences. At the most obvious level, we may all relate to the depressed feeling of being sad, blue, down in the dumps, or low. We have all experienced such feelings in small degrees in our day-to-day living. Less familiar feelings may make no sense to us and in fact may take us aback: low self-esteem and total sense of inadequacy, negating *any* positive attributes or actions that are part of us; total emphasis on our bad qualities; excessive guilt about *everything,* even back to such trivia as a cross word spoken to a friend or teacher twenty years ago. (Of course, as Mormons we are already very good at feeling guilty about all those things we should be doing, or not doing, but the essence of this problem is guilt totally out of proportion to what is real.) We may experience feelings of worthlessness, uselessness, pessimism. We may feel totally helpless and inert, believing that there are no solutions to our pain and that this way of feeling is one for which there is no cure. We might feel a total dissatisfaction with all facets of our lives—hating a job previously well-liked, picking out only faults in our spouse or children. We might lose any and all usual interests (e.g., the formerly active church member who draws into her shell, no longer wanting to associate with others, no longer finding *any* satisfaction in anything). We might experience the sense of not caring about anything, or crying spells for which there seems to be no basis (or feeling like crying much of the time), or feeling out of control—the sense that just now we are really "going crazy." We withdraw and become isolated from family, friends, church. There are shifts in our perception of things such as people's actions or our own image.

Irritability is an extremely common hallmark of depression. In my work in mental health and social services, I see countless cases of true child abuse and neglect, even spouse abuse, that stem from this irritability—feeling out of control, feeling incapable of functioning adequately, or being unable to cope. (Of course, the more positive thing to note here is that many abusive parents can be treated; they can return to their more normal ways of life, and they can keep their children or have them returned.)

A key differential having to do with how we tell when someone is just in a "garden variety" depression as opposed to a significant, clinical depression is the concept of "anhedonia." (This will help us also to distinguish between a normal grief reaction and something that has gone beyond and is more serious.) One of the old schools of philosophy had as its basis the concept of hedonism—the total pursuit of pleasure; hence, "anhedonia," or no pleasure—the *inability* to experience pleasure. This is a crucial point to be aware of. When I am in a minor depression, no matter how poorly I feel most of the time, I am party to moments of excitement, pride, and the like (e.g., at my child's first piano recital). I will for that period of time be able to extend my feelings outside of myself; I will experience real pleasure and satisfaction, and I will forget for at least that time how much the rest of my world may seem to be a failure. In a true, clinical depression, on the other hand, this capacity does not exist, and the extent of my responsiveness may be at best a deadpan, "That's nice, Johnny, I'm glad you did well." Most depressed persons lose their normal sexual drives and feelings, and it is not uncommon for a patient to complain to a counselor, "My wife won't respond to me anymore." There are even cases in which, because of all these symptoms, marital troubles progress so far that needless divorce is the result.

It is important to note that part of virtually any significant depression is the unwanted intrusion of thoughts of death or suicide. This has nothing to do with whether one is a Latter-day Saint or not. In the midst of depressions, Mormons, like people in any other group, may have the strong desire to commit suicide, and some of them do do it. Statistics indicate that one out of two hundred suicide attempts succeeds. And many Latter-day Saints, even knowing that they will come to the other side of the veil with the same problems as now, and with the added burden of being unable to deal with them, are in such pain that they simply cannot handle life. They feel they can no longer inflict their problems on their families or even that the devil has total hold on them and that they must therefore give up. This is tragic, but it happens.

It is important for you to know that you *cannot cause* a person to have suicidal feelings. Since this is part of the depression anyway, most depressed people will only feel relief to have someone ask about these feelings openly. If the person has definite plans, a method, or has tried before, then you will not, of course, want to handle that yourself, but *do* seek out professional help. While the individual may grumble, fight, or push against you, you will have given him the best present a friend or family member can. One last feeling state to be aware of: In severe depressions, thoughts may actually lose contact with reality, and the person becomes what is called psychotic. There may be hallucinations, paranoia, false beliefs (delusions), or worse, even total inability to care for oneself. If we can remember that these are a part of severe depression, they need not be so fearsome.

The second major group of symptoms in the depressive syndrome has to do with a person's cognitive abilities—one's thinking processes. In a depression, it is typical for a person to be completely unable to concentrate, to complain of poor memory, to be unable to follow through on lists or projects, to increase in inaccurate perceptions of just about anything. Because we may not be aware that a person is having these problems unless he is specifically asked, it is worth describing what typical kinds of day-to-day functioning are affected. One group tragically overlooked in the past, but much better diagnosed now, is the elderly. With failing memory and disordered concentration, they may be diagnosed as senile or having dementia. While many forms of senility have no remedy, many of these elderly people are depressed, which is treatable. Teenagers who complain of not doing well in school may be suffering from depression; in fact, a significant number of them will fit this description: unable to concentrate, inattentive to teachers, unable to remember, can't do schoolwork or pass tests, lacking interest in school, truancy, perhaps involved in alcohol or drug abuse, possibly antisocial, even ending up in juvenile court. What a tragedy if these symptoms are missed! The husband or wife at his or her job or housework may be unable to stick to tasks, and there may be an increase in disorganization that results in hours spent in nonproductivity. One may no longer be able to read or even to watch television attentively.

Finally, the third symptom group in depression consists of various physical complaints and problems. A hallmark of depression is sleep disturbance, waking up off and on and waking too early, or (especially in younger age groups) excessive sleep. Appetite change is an additional sign. The most common form is poor appetite with weight loss, but sometimes (again more often among younger age groups) one's appetite and weight may increase dramatically. I have mentioned already the loss of sexual drive, but this too may go to the other extreme. Chronic fatigue, no energy, "dragging," and other such descriptions are probably the best-known symptoms of depression. How many persons go to their family doctor with this complaint? Of course, there are many causes for fatigue that are not related to depression, but too often individuals or physicians neglect the possibility that the fatigue might stem from depression.

Many people suffering from depression will experience what is referred to as "agitation"—an internal feeling of tension, hand wringing, even pacing or hyperactivity; others may be slowed down in all spheres—in speech, walking, and such. Gastrointestinal symptoms are frequent, and constipation or "nervous bowels" may be the result. Frequently nightmares increase. Most people will become preoccupied with their bodily functions in general. And, most important, any and *all* varieties of physical complaint may develop, intensify, or become chronic, especially such things as headaches and muscle tension. If we know the signs, we need not take offense if our family physician can find nothing wrong.

All of these symptoms may be a part of depression. They will come in clusters, and, of course, not all individuals will have exactly the same set, nor will any one individual have all of them. Because of a cultural phenomenon that inhibits the discussion of mental-health problems (we are doing better, but we have a long way to go), most often individuals are reluctant to let others know that they are having these difficulties. As neighbors, family, friends, we need to be aware of some compensating behaviors. Workaholics may be suffering from depression. As they attempt to remove their difficulties by immersing themselves in work, many of these people actually function less effectively, but they are also achieving the social isolation they desire. Acting out behavior in children, teenagers, or adults may be secondary to depression. School difficulties, especially truancy and excessive absenteeism from work may result. An enormous difficulty that may arise from depression is the abuse of alcohol, tobacco, and street drugs, or—much more frequent and somehow more "acceptable" (especially in our LDS culture where it is okay to see a "real" doctor but not a counselor)—abuse of prescription medications to the point of physical addiction that requires hospitalization for withdrawal.

We need not condemn these individuals; all are suffering tremendous pain that has not yet been recognized for what it is. Is it any wonder that they seek relief, even temporarily? (And recall that depression, the "great masquerader," may manifest itself in physical difficulties.) Any major change in a person's functioning may arise from depression. The mother who is no longer able to cope with her kids, who cannot keep up with the housework, who may spend hours in bed, or who becomes the child abuser may be the end product. Realizing that depression does exist will ultimately help us understand our own and others' periods of vulnerability or lessened function.

Causes of Depression

The causes of depression are multiple. Certain personality traits may make us prone to difficulties, yet on the surface these same traits all appear to be admirable—like the ideal Mormon woman: ambitious, hard working, highly goal oriented, a perfectionist, conscientious, highly aware of expectations, getting many jobs done, tending to be hard on oneself, tending toward rigidity. None of these traits on its own would be likely to precipitate a depression; however, any one of them, when combined with a more specific cause, would be experienced as an additional dysfunctional part of our life, a stressor.

The *specific* causes of depression are a little easier to define. Perhaps we may dismiss some 5 to 10 percent as resulting from miscellaneous causes: (1) Physical illness (hypothyroidism, diabetes, certain forms of heart disease, glandular problems, and more "exotic" problems) might appear to be depression or might accompany the symptoms of depression. (2) The phenomena of postpartum depressions, depressions during pregnancy, menopausal depressions, and even our "mini-swings" once a month are all very real physical phenomena that are the result of major hormonal shifts in the body (and therefore in the head). These depressions might occur with more regularity in persons already prone to depression, yet they *are* real and will often respond to appropriate treatment, whether that be through antidepressants or the administration of synthetic hormones. (The depressions related to pregnancy will often resolve themselves.) (3) Certain medications may cause depressions. Birth-control pills are a prime offender. Specific blood-pressure medications, certain forms of steroids, and others may produce the classic symptoms. Of course, in these cases we are lucky: when we withdraw the offending medication, the depression goes away.

Many depressions are *physically* based—those that are referred to as "endogenous" depressions, meaning simply "from within." In these cases of depression (and most experts would describe at least 50 to 75 percent of all cases as endogenous) the individual experiences imbalances of chemicals in the brain that affect his entire physical system in such a way as to produce a major depression with all its concomitant symptoms. This type is thought to be hereditary, for in nearly all individuals, as long as you remember to ask, there will be a history in the family of other persons with problems of depression, "baby blues," suicides, "nervous breakdowns," or alcoholism—a genetic tie for which the reasons are not clear. Typically, these depressions will be precipitated by stress, but there are cases in which no such stressor can be identified; in fact, the depression seems "out of the blue."

The important point to remember concerning endogenous depressions is that they have absolutely *nothing* to do with whether you are a good Mormon living the commandments. A person with this type of depression has an illness, just as we have any other physical illnesses. Such depression can be treated with medications called antidepressants, whose only function is to correct the chemical imbalances that have brought on the symptoms. These are *not* tranquilizers, and they are *not* addicting. An individual treated for this type of depression may have one episode in his life, perhaps one every ten years, or perhaps several times a year. (I have this type myself and feel it is good for people to know that because we often equate "mental illness" with not functioning.) In all cases the medications may be used effectively. In extreme cases, other physical methods may be necessary. The analogy I use with my patients is that as insulin is for the diabetic, so an antidepressant may be for depressions. There is no difference—one is just as real as the other. How sad that many people may go for years and years without the benefit of whatever helps mankind now has available.

And yet how many good, well-meaning, strong members of the Church will respond to such an illness in themselves or others by saying that it is only the result of sin, that they must *do more*, that they are being punished. Such persons would never wince while using the medication prescribed by a "regular" doctor, believing, of course, that these things are meant to be used. Why is it that they cannot conceive of forms of emotional illness that are just as real, have just as much a physical cause, and have just as many means available for overcoming them?

Does it make any sense to believe that we are meant to "gut it out," to avoid the helps that are available, to overcome this "obstacle" in our life only through fasting and prayer?

Surely my own depressions do not indicate to me that I am wicked, sinful, or bad. Rather, I choose to look upon this as one more fact that I have learned about my own body, and because of this knowledge I can then choose to do something about it and control the problem. Yes, I have needed to overcome it— but it did not happen until I used *all* modalities that were necessary. So many Latter-day Saints have problems with this concept. When it comes to emotional difficulties, we too often view them as weaknesses, defects, or a result of some other negative trait. For myself, I know that God provided all the knowledge, all the tools. To say that antidepressant medications should not be used because they are "of this world" makes no sense to me, for I know that *all* knowledge comes from God as we are ready to receive it.

In a documentary on a public television station not long ago, a group of researchers were discussing the discovery of antidepressants and similar medications. None of these people were Mormon. In fact, many were not sure of any belief. But all indicated that the "accidents" that led to the discoveries occurred "almost as if we were being led." Now you and I know that these were no accidents. God gives us knowledge continually—knowledge that we are meant to use, make sense of, and not keep hidden under our bushel.

The final major cause of depression is defined most often as being of a "reactive" nature. This type is what most people think of when they think of any form of depression, that is, the depression that results from responses or reactions to some life event, usually some form of loss. Losses may be of many different types, and the loss need not be an actual, tangible thing. Losses may be as varied as the death of a loved one, sending one's son or daughter on a mission, losing a business position or promotion, or the like. In fact, in the Church the intangible losses are much more often our major source of difficulty— such things as losing our self-esteem, feeling a loss as we recognize that gap between what we expect of ourselves (or others), and what we see ourselves (or others) actually doing. We may feel an acute loss if we are not living up to the standards of the Church. We may even feel a loss of the control of our lives if, in our misinterpretation of church teachings, we feel that our individuality and unique ways of doing things must be submerged in total obedience to the least of church doctrines. These types of losses are just as real as any death or tangible difficulty; in fact, they may be much harder to overcome because we do not see before us specific problems we can tackle. In any case, losses produce stress or depression.

Treatment consists of what most of us call therapy. It is important to know that there are many different approaches and many different types of professionals who can provide assistance to the individual. Because people vary so much, it is not necessary to feel that any one approach to therapy is the only way. What will ultimately be of the greatest importance will be to work with someone with whom you may feel comfortable, can develop trust, and who will allow himself some flexibility with you along the way. Some bishops are excellent counselors; many family doctors will take the extra time to work with a depressed patient. Usually these individuals will sense when a problem is beyond their capacity to handle and will refer it elsewhere. However, if this does not happen, or if a specific professional counselor does not seem to be meeting our needs, let us never forget that here, as in any other aspect of our life, we have free agency, the right to change, to pursue church lines of authority to our satisfaction in order to obtain the help we need.

There will commonly be some overlap between reactive and endogenous forms of depression. Thus, most persons with a known heredity of depressive illness will seek therapy in conjunction with appropriate physical treatment. After all, insofar as we have stresses in our lives and may have learned ineffectual patterns of response or behavior, and insofar as these may precipitate the biological swing, it is worth the effort to learn how to cope with stress and to unlearn those difficulties that may be leaving us more open to depression.

As women in the Church, we are probably subject to some

special forms of vulnerability to stress and depression. Part of this vulnerability results from the simple fact that we *are* women, which, of course, means the problem is not restricted to our church. Nevertheless, in the Mormon culture, with our usual prescription of roles and models for functioning and thinking about ourselves, which in many cases are perceived as rigid and unbending, we become increasingly vulnerable. This cultural vulnerability is probably most closely bound with ways in which we learn to define ourselves as we grow and with the sorts of things we may come to expect or want for ourselves and those about us. A recent book by Silvano Arieti (*Severe and Mild Depression,* New York: Basic Books, 1978) perhaps gives us our clearest treatment of the problem as it explores how people may spend their lives living for what he calls a "dominant other." A dominant other may be your husband, your job, or a set of things you believe you should be doing, and if you find yourself not living in harmony with this dominant other, you lose this measure with which to define yourself.

Perhaps we may consider a graphic, unfortunately common illustration of how such a vulnerability might come about. Let us postulate a prospective Patti Perfect. Patti Jr. has been born and raised in Tinytown, Utah. Her father is the bishop of her ward, her mother is the Relief Society president, and her uncle down the block is the stake president. Patti's small town is approximately 98 percent Mormon, and she has never really learned to understand that there are other people on this earth who exist without the influence of the gospel in their lives. Patti has been raised to believe that anything a bishop, stake president, even a Relief Society board member, may say (on *any* subject, mind you) is absolute gospel truth. Patti's entire life plan has been made for her since at least the age of three when she first learned to say "celestial." She will graduate from high school and will have a husband in the wings or, in lieu thereof, will continue on at BYU (not particularly to learn or develop a talent or career, but to find the elusive returned missionary who will take her to the temple, place her on a pedestal, and provide her total security in life). She will marry, have six children, and carry at least four high positions in the Church. And she will live happily ever after. Now you can imagine in this plan what innumerable pitfalls and traps have been set. Patti has learned to define herself and her life in terms of attributes or events totally outside her control. Patti believes that if she does not marry, she must be unworthy and a failure. If she marries, has her six children, but then feels unhappy, she will experience a major loss in terms of unfulfilled expectations; she will, however, worsen her own situation by believing that because she feels this, she is guilty. The "Church" has promised her that these things will make her happy, and surely if she is not, the fault is hers; an underlying sin *must* be preventing her progression. Patti has been taught to regard herself as worthwhile *only* insofar as she is as a mother, a wife, and an active church participant, and certainly only insofar as she approaches the status of a senior Patti Perfect.

But what about those of us who may not marry in this life? What of those wives who find they are unable to bear children? What of the countless numbers in our midst who really try to do the 150 or more things each day, only to find themselves unappreciated, neglected, or unhappy? These are individuals whose very existence is not of their own making. And what if they have never learned to define themselves solely in terms of their own intrinsic worth? What a tragedy—especially when we find it in our Church, for we have the perfect perspectives and teachings to show us the foolhardy nature of such assumptions. We alone, in the Church, have a sure knowledge of the true plan of salvation. No other people on earth can better comprehend our place in the premortal existence, our choice to come to this earth, the risks we promised to take by living, and our sense that despite it all, we may live confidently and patiently no matter what our trial. If we truly adhere to the things we learn through the Church, none of us should lose our hold on the iron rod.

"I am a child of God." "I have intrinsic worth." "I have a track record already—I was not one of the third that perished before the world began." "I am a good person." How is it that these concepts, so easily accepted and acted upon by us as children, somehow shift as we become adults? You have seen the little five-year-old girl in her new lace dress, looking the picture of innocence and openness. To this little human being you may say, "You look so nice today" and she will respond, "I know!" How horrified we would be if this experience were repeated with an adult! Somewhere in our lives we seem to learn that it is not okay to have good feelings about ourselves, to accept compliments readily from those around us, or to say "I am good; I do that well." We brand that as conceit, pride, or vanity. We have forgotten somehow that we do have that intrinsic worth and not only can but should develop and grow for ourselves, not for another person or an outside cause. If we plan our lives according to the latter framework, our reward will be only disappointment and depression. To spend our lives doing what we do for another person is to make certain our vulnerability to loss, to disappointment, to depression. People outside ourselves are not predictable—*that* is one thing that *is* predictable! (The sole exception to this rule is the Lord, Jesus Christ. His expectations for us will never lead us astray and will never vary.)

We have looked at expectations and at the resulting imbalance. We have mentioned the kinds of losses we may experience. However, I believe that our greatest vulnerability in the Church results from our tendency to apply doctrinal issues to our lives without ever really thinking about them. The result is a mass of confusion and misinterpretation that true study of gospel principles could have prevented. Perhaps the classic example of this point is to be found in this tired assertion, "If you're good, you'll have blessings. If you're bad, you won't." In the eternities, in the course of our eternal lives, the argument is absolutely valid; but no one with the authority to do so has ever said that if we are good today we will have blessings today, or that if we are good we will not have sorrow. How amazed I am to find this an overriding belief among a sad majority of Church members. But they have set the traps themselves, for somehow they convert the general principle to these ideas: (1) If this bad thing happens to me, it means that I have been bad and am being punished. (2) If things are going well for me, it means that I must be doing right. (3) As long as I do well, I will never have real cause for sorrow and bad things will not befall me. Perhaps the most fundamental doctrine of our Church is the concept of free agency—yet all these assumptions would seek to negate this principle, to take away experiences that ultimately may be the source of our greatest growth and progression.

I was in a Relief Society meeting when one sister told of an experience with a leader who said, "Women who get depressed just do not have a testimony." Once my blood cools, I can only hope to find this leader, vicariously at least, to confront her with the absolute incompatibility of her statement with church teachings. If I could talk with such a person, I would go back to the beginning and talk about the premortal existence in this way: "Back in the preexistence there were two plans. In the first plan we were told that we would have the opportunity to live on earth, that we would have no choice, and that we would have essentially instant feedback on all that we did—good would immediately beget good, bad bad. In this plan we might have a comfortable life, but surely we would experience no challenge nor any opportunity to grow. The second plan gave mankind the choice to live this life. We were told that our lives might not always be pleasant but that we would be expected to 'roll with the punches.' We would know the essence of sorrow because we know its opposite—joy. And we were told that we would not be left without direction, but that to obtain it *we* would have to initiate the contact." Then I would ask said individual, "Which plan do you think your ideas sound more like?"

Our friend might be taken aback, but her notions are consistent with the idea of instant feedback. Perhaps she would be harder to convince. The next conversation would then go: "You believe that President Kimball is a prophet, right? That on earth he is the closest thing we have to a man living in a state of perfection, being spiritually in tune, and holding his life in obedience to the will of the Father? Well, what you are saying is that deep underneath, in the depths of his soul, President Kimball is a wicked and sinful man!" How could I say this to her? Many of us have read the prophet's biography. We are aware of his many trials—the loss of parents, severe illnesses when young, the attacks of Bell's palsy, the throat cancer, the heart attacks, and the problems with the subdurals. Yet this individual at my side would have me believe that for those difficulties to befall the prophet he must be a wicked man, that otherwise he would be "living in a bed of roses."

How many other day-to-day examples can we think of that are merely outgrowths of our rigid friend's assumptions? In the KSL program, one woman (a bishop's wife, no less) told how she was *not* helped by the nurse who said, "Oh, if you had only read your scriptures more, this wouldn't have happened." Why are we so hard to convince when the principles are so fundamental? I might be living every commandment of the gospel to the very best of my ability, but if I experience an episode of endogenous depression, I could do little to end it—except to recognize it and get help. In depression, the person already feels guilty, so how can it help to heap extra guilt upon ourselves by accepting the idea that our depression results from our actions? This cycle will only lead the individual to despair.

Another graphic example of how we as members should *not* approach a brother or sister in distress or pain is in the book of Job. Job, who is in a deep clinical depression (he describes his sense of hopelessness, helplessness, his constant suicidal thoughts, his loss of appetite, his poor sleep), is visited by three well-meaning friends, Eliphaz, Bildad, and Zophar, who seek to comfort him by lecturing and trying to justify his fallen state. In the responses of these three individuals, we can see every fallacy that so many would seek to use in "helping" others cope with depression: (1) You must not have been living in tune with the Lord despite all your outside appearances. Surely you know that no good or innocent person would ever be punished. Your best course will be to go, confess your sins, and expect the Lord's miracle to you. (See Job 4.) (2) Really, you should not express these negative feelings at all. Remember that we are to "rejoice in all things." If a man truly has God as part of his life, he will continually be filled with laughter and shouts of joy. (See Job 8.) (3) There must be a secret sin in your life. God is doubtless punishing you far less than you deserve. (See Job 11.) (4) Your pride has brought you low. "Pride cometh before the fall." (See Job 15.) (5) You just don't know God. Otherwise you could accept and understand all these things.

(See Job 18.) (6) God has finally caught up with you for your past. (See Job 20.) (7) The feelings that you are expressing only prove that you "have had it coming." You really have been a hypocrite all along. (See Job 22.) (8) You have not lived your life in total dependence on God. You have not realized that you cannot function in your own strengths but must depend completely upon God. (See Job 25.)

These ideas are, of course, all paraphrased, and I am indebted for their emphasis to a nameless Christian pastor whose radio broadcast I heard by accident. But the point is that at the last God rebukes the three "friends," telling them that they have not represented him correctly, nor his teachings or his ways of dealing with mankind. (See Job 42.) I doubt that we could find a more straightforward message addressing the hurtful effects of individual misinterpretation.

An additional immense source of vulnerability for us has to do with the problems of anger. There exists a wonderful organization to which I belong, called the Association of Mormon Counselors and Psychotherapists (AMCAP). Our membership consists of counselors and other professionals who meet at least twice each year in conjunction with general conference. In our October meetings I had the opportunity to work with an individual, Burton Kelly, of the Counseling Center at BYU, who gave an enormously helpful workshop on the use of the scriptures as an adjunct in therapy. Following his workshop, I spent some time with him requesting additional scriptural references that deal with the problems of anger. I could find numerous examples of males becoming angry, but I was not sufficiently expert in the scriptures to know of examples for females.

Not having received a reply since that time, I was dismayed to open my February 1980 *Ensign* to a four-page article called "The Case Against Anger," written by this same good brother. All the points made in his article are valid, but they are valid for perhaps one-third of all the reasons for which individuals become angry and *not* for the other two-thirds. The trouble with this sort of approach is that people such as Patti Jr., from Tinytown, Utah, will read the article, and believe that anything published in the *Ensign* represents *the* gospel truth from month to month, and never thereafter ponder its content or really stop to think of its implications for themselves. If Patti Jr. had come to one of my workshops and begun to feel a little better about anger, she would now just as easily feel, "Well, I heard Sister Hirsh, but I guess what she told us is not true—and anyway, she doesn't have the priesthood, so it all must have been a pack of lies!" And that is too bad. The points of the article are valid; appropriate treatments are suggested for the times when anger is not necessary or may not be a useful response. Unfortunately, though, these points will be drowned out by the overshadowing message that all anger results *from* sin and that all anger results *in* sin. But is this really true? What about anger that results from such day-to-day feelings as disappointments, lost expectations, not seeing ourselves live up to our thoughts? Brother Kelly defines anger as arising only when one is judging another person or comparing himself; this negates all of the kinds of anger that most of us in the Church (and in the world in general) experience the most.

In the Church we seem to have an exceedingly difficult time with our anger; we have the unspoken message that anger is something one should never feel, show, or acknowledge in any way. Unfortunately, a significant group of those who become depressed do so because buried within them is so much anger that they have never been able to express. Anger is, in addition to an emotion, a real physical, chemical response, and that energy must be dissipated in some way. If it is not, the individual may turn it against himself in the form of emotional difficulty or even of physical illness. Why is this such a difficult concept for us in the Church? In trying to address the problem of anger, I tend to pull out of my hat such questions as, "Remember the flood?" Or what of Christ in the temple as he drove out the money changers? I do not imagine that at that time Christ was in a state of meekness and peace; rather, I suspect he must have been feeling immense anger at these people and hurt to see them defile his Father's house. Joseph Smith, as he spent his hours in Liberty Jail, became angry at God, saying in effect, "I can take no more of this! How long must it go on? Can't you give the people a break?" (See D&C 121.) (Note that in response to Joseph's anger, God filled him with words of comfort and patience that no doubt were of great benefit to Joseph.) I submit to us all: If God and Christ and Joseph Smith can be angry, does it make any sense to say that we cannot? In Brother Kelly's article, he deals with this issue by saying that they were not angry, that what they were feeling was probably something "higher" that we in our human frailty cannot understand but choose to call anger.

Now, I am not the final authority on the gospel. Each of us will have to receive his own witness of these things. But as far as I am concerned, an important part of the ministry of Christ and of all our teachers is to show us their humanness—to show us that they have these feelings and can use them constructively. Because Christ used his anger wisely, he was able to avert the stoning of the adulterous woman. I believe God must have been very angry at the time he caused the flood—probably feeling as torn up and frustrated as any father toward his children.

For persons who may be having a struggle with this, there is a way out that I use commonly in therapy, especially with couples and families. This alternative is based on the fact that anger is a superficial emotion. It is always a secondary response, although we seldom acknowledge this fact. It is the *result* of other feelings, and we would be using our efforts more constructively if we were attempting to define what feelings lie beneath the anger—feelings such as hurt, rejection, disappointment, and defeat. (We might speculate that Christ had such feelings as dismay and disappointment or hurt for his Father as he saw the people not understanding his truths.)

Consider, for example, the tired wife who is greeted by her husband who comes in the door, throws his briefcase down in the hall, and heads for the living room to read the evening paper and put his feet up. The wife has two ways of responding. If she comes up with something like, "You never come home to see *me*. You never help me in the kitchen. You always have to be selfish and read the paper," she will only put her husband on the defensive, and she will feel out of control. She will not have told him what she needed; all she will have done is to vent the secondary response of anger. How much more useful it would be for her to say, "You know, honey, when you come home from work and go to the living room that way, it really hurts me. I feel that you must not even care enough about me to ask about my day. It makes me feel neglected. Could you spend more time with me when you first come home? Probably both of us have had a hard day and could use each other's support." What a breakthrough! Here the wife has vented her true feelings. Neither party will feel hurt in this exchange; instead each has the opportunity to grow closer to the other. Anger is a real feeling. It must not be buried, but it can be used to accomplish constructive ends. If we bury it, we are only asking for difficulty and increasing our vulnerability.

By now it should be obvious that the concept of there being only one way to do things is not always productive. Stemming from this are the questions, "What happens when we overdo in our church roles?" and "How do we say no?" I have seen blackboards filled with lists of what Mormon women thought they should be doing. But what happens when we reach our saturation point? When should we say no, and how do we deal with this? Many of us then feel guilty; yet if we do not, we end up feeling swamped, put upon, and eventually depressed. If we do not deal evenly and thoughtfully with problems such as this, we lose our balance.

Maintaining Balance

We have looked at depression, what it is like, our vulnerabilities, and the ways that we can get help. We can to some degree avoid depression, or at least cope with it. The determining factor is how we keep balance in our lives—and this will be the focus for the remainder of my discussion. We have a great many ways in which we can be of help to ourselves. The number of books, lay articles, and the like produced in recent years is truly gratifying, and I am always happy to provide individuals with such references as they desire. Brother Kelly provided us a marvelous handout at the same AMCAP conference last fall listing basic therapy principles found in the scriptures. (See p. 180.) How wonderful it is to look at these concepts and to see that, contrary to what many Latter-day Saints feel about psychotherapy (that it is just one step up from witchcraft), the teachings and principles have been with us all along. Much time must be spent in virtually all therapy situations helping the individual to learn to love and feel good about himself—an attitude that so many persons see as sinful and selfish. Yet Christ taught us to love our neighbor *as* ourselves, *not* before, instead of, or after. I doubt that it is possible for any of us to love another person openly and fully unless we first believe in ourselves, love ourselves, and have the conviction of our own worth.

But what must we Latter-day Saints do to maintain our balance or to help ourselves if we are having the emotional difficulties and illnesses we have described? Are there things that we may do to keep ourselves from falling in the first place? For me, balance in the Church has several facets. The first, I feel, is to understand who and what we are. In that same fall AMCAP conference, we had an exceptional workshop given by Dr. Sterling Ellsworth, a psychologist practicing in Eugene, Oregon. In this workshop Dr. Ellsworth introduced to us the concept of the two selves that exist in all of us. This idea is not new. Freud spoke of the base, undisciplined id and the strict superego, and today we hear of the OK and not OK selves. Yet taken in the gospel context, this concept makes wonderful sense and can really help us conceptualize many things that may have confused us. These two selves consist, first, of our true self, which is obviously our spirit self. This part of each of us, which is positive, smart, and open, is what we are given when we are born. The child, who comes into the world pure in spirit, is unblemished and uncluttered and has not yet learned the fallacies and mixed messages so typical of the world. What then is our negative self? This is the accumulation of all those unproductive things that we learn by default as we grow in this life, those parts of us we recognize as "clutter" or our "garbage piles."

The messages we get from this part of us are: "You aren't worth it. You shouldn't think good things about yourself. You *must* and you can meet all of your needs only from outside yourself." These responses are *all* learned and, of course, are authored by the father of all lies. It is these aspects of our negative self, not our true spirit self, that create in us our problems and our inabilities to cope.

Think about this—it clarifies so many doctrines that otherwise might be incomprehensible. Take, for example, the concept of unconditional love. Do you ever find it impossible to get up in front of hundreds of people and say, so that you mean it, "I *love* all of you"? I have this problem. I might not even know the majority of the people. How then can I love them? But when I realize that we are kindred spirits and have known and cared for each other all along, I can say that I love them all. I may not be able to say that I like what they do, but my spirit can reach out to love all of their spirits. In this context I can also catch some glimpse of what God's unconditional love for each of us is like, and I can be more open to experience human examples that illustrate this for me.

Let me use a personal experience to illustrate how I was able to comprehend this principle. This incident occurred while I was working with my own therapist at a time when I was dealing with some particularly difficult issues in my life. I had finally trusted this one individual enough to try to talk with him concerning things that I had never before really been able to tell anyone and had carried about as part of my own personal "garbage pile" for years. Then, as I talked and was somehow feeling that I would never really be able to look this person in the eye again, I heard sniffing. Looking up, I saw this wonderful person with eyes red and face flushed. Incredulous, I could only whisper, "Are you crying?" When I received an affirmative answer and asked how this could be, he responded, "It hurts me to see you feeling so bad and then being so hard on yourself." Ever since then, I think I have been able to imagine how God must feel when we sin. I don't think that he sits up there being angry with us; probably he looks down and feels very sad—and hurts for us because of how we hurt ourselves.

For me, balance within the Church entails understanding how the Church really does give us a working frame of reference in which we may sensibly build our lives. In the Church we are truly blessed. We have Christ, and our special understanding of him gives us all the focus we need for our existence.

Christ is no doubt the best psychotherapist who ever lived, because he represents all those qualities and the empathic approach that bring out the best in people.

In that same AMCAP conference, Stephen R. Covey spoke on how keeping Christ as the center of our lives helps us focus our attention properly and how everything else then falls into place. According to Brother Covey, Christ provides all the dimensions needed to maximize our human growth and understanding. The first dimension is security. Insofar as Christ gives us that—because he provides us with our knowledge of self and supports our individual uniqueness—we need never fall into despair. Knowing that we are children of God and that we are worth something can give each of us perhaps the greatest single source of hope for surviving any problem that befalls us in this life. The second dimension is guidance. Christ, the scriptures, and the gospel teachings (the real ones—not individual interpretations) give us the very best standards for dealing with ourselves and others. (In searching for references for this talk I found a book titled "Bible Therapy." It was written by a Christian minister, but the basic principles are correct. Maybe we as Latter-day Saints need no longer be afraid to take a look at our problems and admit that we are human. Then such books will come from our own!) Third, Christ's wisdom provides the perfect model of balance. Christ acknowledged his own weaknesses and did not shrink from wrestling with them. In the Garden of Gethsemane Christ was anguished, feeling fear and uncertainty as he contemplated the suffering to come. But by acknowledging this weakness and by praying with all his might for help and strength, he was able to say calmly, "Nevertheless, not my will, but thine." Given the example of Christ, who are we to say we cannot admit to weakness? Finally, Christ gives us power in our lives. We have this power from knowing of his very real love and support for us, and we may use this power as we teach and try to be an influence for good among others.

Now, in real-life, practical terms, what will keep us in balance? Here are the things I have come up with. Many of you will want to add your own.

1. *Think rather than be a blind sheep.* This remains my

number-one message to the people of the Church. Let us think about what we are taught. A principle is of no use if we have not developed our own witness of its truthfulness. If we read the writings of the prophets, we will find each of them saying that if we are only following the crowd, we are no better than that person who has never heard the gospel at all. If we are willfully blind, we cause our own problems. Use your free agency—that is why you have it.

2. *Keep your expectations realistic.* None of us can ever really be Patti Perfect—there simply are not enough hours in the day. If this is what we set up for ourselves, we are bound to be disappointed. That was never what the Lord or the teachings of the Church intended.

3. *Look at guidelines for what they are.* Guidelines are not the same as "thou shalts." We have not been given a commandment to bake twelve loaves of bread this day, knit four booties the next, and the like. These are goals for us to strive for. We should always remember Barbara Smith's excellent admonition to us: "Remember, goals are stars to steer by, not sticks with which to beat ourselves." Maybe there are so many different and varied guidelines available to us because *we* are so many. We all have very different interests, talents, feelings, and capabilities. Consequently, no one set of guidelines could possibly pertain to us all. I may not be able to quilt (even if I'd love to learn), but I can do things that others cannot. When we see these massive lists of things to do, we need to consider the possibility that the list is great and diverse so that each of us can comfortably find our niche somewhere within, not that each of us is required to do absolutely everything.

4. *Allow yourself your humanness and your feelings.* This we all must do for our own mental health. And by applying the principles as parents, teachers, and counselors, we can administer some real preventive medicine. There is nothing wrong with having any feeling, even the negative ones. When people learn to express themselves in terms of feelings, there is no possibility for defensiveness, misunderstanding, or hurt. (Recall the wife and her husband at the end of the day.) If we teach ourselves and our children the importance of feelings—

and of using them constructively—we lay a solid groundwork for a healthy sense of self-esteem and provide the best opportunity for continuing growth in all spheres. Perhaps children taught in this way would grow up to be wonderful, open adults without many of the problems we have. Using our humanness is the soundest policy. Recall how human Christ was—and how perfect he became. This helps me grow better than if I think in terms of "I'm not supposed to have such feelings."

5. *Seek the Spirit in all things.* This is critical in our lives. If we seek the Spirit, we will not be blind sheep but will be in control of the important aspects of our lives. If I have a truly important decision to make, if I have something weighing heavy on my mind, or if there seems to be a conflict between something that is asked of me and my own problems and concerns, I need to consider that the conflict might have been given to me for my growth. In thinking this way, I will be bound to seek the Spirit and get my own guidance. Doctrine and Covenants section 50 teaches us that the Spirit does not contradict itself. If you have not read that marvelous book by Blaine Yorgason, *Charlie's Monument,* read it. That really shows the ways of using the Holy Spirit to resolve our trials.

6. *Choose how you will serve in the Church.* Richard Cummings has said that too often we end up *losing* ourselves in the Church when really we were meant to find ourselves. And I have heard marvelous talks given by Lynn Scoresby, a Latter-day Saint psychologist, on how service in the Church can ruin our marriages if carried to excess. In all things it is critical that we remember our priorities. If, knowing that home and family are my first priority, I obtain a testimony that one more church assignment would work a hardship on my family, I am justified in saying no. No bishop in the Church, if he truly understands our circumstances and heart and prays about these things himself, will ask of us a thing that is not right. Or if he does ask it, and we appropriately let him know of our concerns, he will not try to force us to carry through. A woman who had recently recovered from a very deep and long-standing depression found herself wanting further growth and development in the Church. Lo and behold, within a week her bishop called her to

be president of the choir. Because this would have been her fourth consecutive music job, this woman—my friend—felt a mixture of pleasure and anguish. After thinking about it, she told her bishop of her need to grow, that she would be happy to take the calling, that she loved music and would always be willing to serve in the Church, but that it probably would not afford her the greatest potential for progression. She also gave the bishop the names of twelve persons in the ward—unknown to him—who could work with music. You can guess the happy results. A week later this sister was asked to teach in the Sunday School, and the choir job went elsewhere. This good bishop echoed a great truth to my friend when he said, "I can be inspired only insofar as I have the knowledge. If I do not know of your needs and circumstances, I cannot best fill your and the Church's needs." What a great truth. Bishops are human too—we ought not to assume that they can read our minds.

7. *Allow yourself your own progression.* We are here to *grow.*

8. *Assume personal responsibility.* In therapy we help people by making them aware of their own capacities to solve problems, not by doing it for them. Ultimately, none of us may be responsible for anyone other than ourselves. No person can ever force another to do his bidding, have his thoughts, or respond his way. If we know this, we have our best chance for growth.

9. *Become as a child.* This we *must* do to inherit the kingdom. But why is this so? In the Primary song "I Am a Child of God," the childlike qualities are listed: meekness, mildness, humility. Then add goodness, openness, and so on. The child becomes meek and mild in the same way that we keep in balance. The qualities are all that we have been talking of: being open and able to change and think, developing, growing, not having preconceived ideas, being uncluttered, believing in ourselves as special, believing that we can truly do things—as the therapy phrase goes ("I am lovable and capable"). To become as a child is to have these things as part of our being and hence to keep in balance.

10. *Remember that God provides the knowledge and the*

means that people are using nowadays to help you. We need not shun therapy, counseling, or medication because it is "manmade." Women in my office have wept openly at the idea of taking a medication (or using it on their child). They ask, "If I use this, will I really be doing my job at overcoming this thing? Am I not supposed to suffer more?" I wish I could say this is made up, but it is not. I hope the mere suggestion that this is so very foolish and tragic can be considered by us all.

11. *Don't be afraid to get help.* This is what this entire talk has been about. And remember that help comes in many forms.

12. *Don't be afraid to say no.* We have looked at this already. There *are* times when the no with which you respond is far more responsible than a mindless, passive yes.

13. *Get in touch with your own sense of self-esteem.* Preventive medicine is the name of the game for us, our families, and our friends and loved ones. And part of that medicine is learning to love and respect ourselves.

14. *Learn to laugh at yourself.* The ability to laugh at ourselves is one of the healthiest traits we can develop. If parents learn to laugh at themselves, their children will laugh with them, not at them.

15. *Learn to be gentle with yourself.* None of us is really sufficient in this sphere, but each of us can find individual helps, writings, and other sources that will lift us and help us cope. I think my favorites within the Church are the writings of Paul Dunn. They give us perspective gently and positively while addressing real, everyday tragedies and problems. The message is that what matters is our continuing to try. When my therapist said, "Well, I guess I identify with the struggle," I could understand how he could still love me even knowing my deepest faults. That is the essence of Christ's mission on this earth.

In summary, let us each do our best to maintain some balance and perspective in our life. You may have seen the newspaper captions called "In the Mind's Eye." My favorite shows an enormous tree that has been toppled in a storm, and the caption reads, "Handle problems as they come. Even a large tree is easily moved one piece at a time." May we all try to keep this in mind. I leave with you my testimony that this church affords us the greatest opportunity for achieving balance and serenity in our lives.

Successfully Coping with Stress: Solutions from the Scriptures

1. I will not let my heart be troubled; as I think in my heart so am I; I will think truths. (John 14:1, 27; Proverbs 23:7.)
2. I create my own stresses; therefore, I can uncreate and prevent them by living the laws of peace. (D&C 130:20-21; John 10:1; Luke 2:13-14; 2 Timothy 1:7.)
3. I will prepare myself well for my responsibilities so that I shall not fear. (D&C 38:30; Isaiah 57:20-21.)
4. I will develop increasing love for others and myself so that my confidence might wax strong. (D&C 121:45-46; Matthew 22:36-40; Romans 14:22; Moroni 8:16.)
5. I can do no better today than my today's best; my best tomorrow will be better. (2 Nephi 28:30.)
6. I believe in *becoming* perfect; I also believe in the law of eternal progression. (President Joseph Fielding Smith.)
7. I will do all things in order and be diligent, but not attempt to run faster nor labor more than I have strength. (D&C 10:4; Mosiah 4:27.)
8. For my sins I will have Godly sorrow that leads to repentance, not the sorrow of the world; I will keep my eye on the next time, not the last time. (2 Corinthians 7:10.)
9. I will remember to live by "want to" rather than "have to." (2 Nephi 2:26-27; Helaman 14:30-31; D&C 58:26-29.)
10. I am responsible for my behavior, but I cannot and will not attempt to control the behavior of others. (D&C 121:41; Moses 4:1-2; Ezekiel 18:4, 14-20; 33:7-9.)
11. I will live the spirit of the Word of Wisdom. (D&C 89; 88:124; Luke 2:52.)
12. I will focus my life on the Savior, learn of him, become "meek and lowly in heart," and I shall have peace in him. (D&C 10:23; Matthew 11:28-30.)

Libby R. Hirsb has a bachelor's degree from Northwestern University, a master's in clinical psychology from the University of Kansas, and an M.D. from the University of Chicago. A psychiatrist, she is associated with a mental health center in the Salt Lake City area.

Reading and Loving
Literature

MARILYN ARNOLD

A stanza in a poem called "Miniver Cheevy" by Edwin Arlington Robinson goes like this: "Miniver scorned the gold he sought,/But sore annoyed he was without it./Miniver thought, and thought, and thought,/And thought, and thought about it."[1] I know how he feels. I have thought, and thought, and thought about this assignment, trying to decide how academic or personal to make it. I decided finally to go the personal route, realizing that I cannot really persuade you to love literature by arguing you into it. I can only tell you how I feel about it, read to you a few of the things that I love, and hope that something will be stirred within you that will result in a greater appreciation for literature.

Thoreau said in the beginning of *Walden,* "In most books, the 'I' or first person is omitted; in this it will be retained; that in respect to egotism, is the main difference. We commonly do not remember that it is, after all, always the first person that is speaking. I should not talk so much about myself if there were anybody else whom I knew as well."[2] So I'm borrowing Thoreau's rationale: I would talk about someone else and someone else's loves if I knew as much about them as I do about my own.

We literature teachers are often asked questions like this: "Why should we take this class?" "Why should we read this book?" "Why should we trouble ourselves over poetry?" "Of what possible use is it?" What our questioners are really asking is, "How will appreciating literature help me get that second car or that job in the bank?" We tend to think of things as being useful only if they have some kind of economic value. For me, the most valuable things in this world do not have price tags; they cannot be assigned material value. They are things that speak to the heart and the mind and the spirit and that do something for us in ways we cannot measure. Literature is one of those things.

We commonly say that the thing that separates the lower animals from human beings is that human beings have an innate capacity for reason. I think there is another distinction just as important—and just as innate. I call it, for lack of a better term, the aesthetic sense. Have you ever seen a cow get excited about a sunset? Or a dog go into ecstasy over a flower or a painting? Willa Cather said once that she had never been able to impress a cow in a Nebraska pasture with one of her sonnets yet, and she did not expect ever to be able to. Animals do have feelings, of course, and an appreciation for movement. I skied to school yesterday, and a young German shepherd decided to accompany me. He rollicked and frolicked through all the deepest drifts, obviously having a marvelous time; but I could have recited a poem to him and he would not have been impressed at all, I am sure.

We remember that the Savior told us he came to earth so that we might have life "more abundantly." I do not believe that he was interpreting the abundant life in terms of recreational vehicles, boats, or color television sets. Knowing the kind of value system that he represented, we can assume that he was talking about a more abundant spiritual life, intellectual life, and emotional life. I believe that artists—musicians, painters, writers—are no accident. They are created to bless our lives.

Now I would like to make some general suggestions about reading literature. First, when you approach a piece of literature, simply love it for its own sake. Do not try to find uses for it—just relish it. Let the words and the rhythm have their way with you, and let the work fill your mind with the richness of its language, the wonder of its conception. Here are a few examples of beauty that is, as Emerson says, "its own excuse for being." This first one is from a Shakespearean play, *Antony and Cleopatra*. It contains a marvelous scene in which Cleopatra is described as she arrives by barge on the river. She is adorned voluptuously—she would have to be—in magnificent trappings. This is how Enobarbus, one of the characters in the play, describes her:

> The barge she sat in, like a burnish'd throne,
> Burn'd on the water: The poop was beaten gold;
> Purple the sails, and so perfumed that
> The winds were love-sick with them; the oars were silver,
> Which to the tune of flutes kept stroke and made
> The water which they beat to follow faster,
> As amorous of their strokes. For her own person,
> It beggar'd all description: she did lie
> In her pavilion, cloth-of-gold tissue,
> O'er-picturing that Venus where we see
> The fancy outwork nature: on each side her
> Stood pretty dimpled boys, like smiling Cupids,
> With divers-colour'd fans, whose wind did seem
> To glow the delicate cheeks which they did cool,
> And what they undid did.
> Her gentlewomen, like the Nereides,
> So many mermaids, tender her i' the eyes,
> And made their bends adornings: at the helm
> A seeming mermaid steers: the silken tackle
> Swell with the touches of those flower-soft hands,
> That yarely frame the office. From the barge
> A strange invisible perfume hits the sense
> Of the adjacent wharfs. The city cast
> Her people out upon her; and Antony,
> Enthron'd i' the market-place, did sit alone,
> Whistling to the air; which, but for vacancy,
> Had gone to gaze on Cleopatra too,
> And made a gap in nature.[3]

Another example of this kind of writing is found in a passage from *Death Comes for the Archbishop*, by Willa Cather. This is a novel about a French priest who has been sent to the desolate New Mexico territory to establish the church on firm footing there. He is a cultured, refined man, and it was expected that he would return to France when he retired. But during his final visit to France before his retirement, something happens to him. He decides that he cannot stay in France. He must live out his life on the desert. (Those of you who love the desert as I do will understand his need.) Cather describes his feelings:

> In the Old World he found himself homesick for the New. It was a feeling he could not explain; a feeling that old age did not weigh so heavily on a man in New Mexico as in the Puy-de-Dôme.
>
> He loved the towering peaks of his native mountains, the comeliness of the villages, the cleanness of the country-side. . . . When the summer wind stirred the lilacs in the old gardens and shook down the blooms of the horse-chestnuts, he sometimes closed his eyes and thought of the high song the wind was singing in the straight, striped pine trees up in the Navajo forests.
>
> During the day his nostalgia wore off, and by dinner-time it was quite gone. He enjoyed his dinner and his wine, and the company of cultivated men, and usually retired in good spirits. It was in the early morning that he felt the ache in his breast; it had something to do with waking in the early morning. It seemed to him that the grey dawn lasted so long here, the country was a long time in coming to life. The gardens and the fields were damp, heavy mists hung in the valley and obscured the mountains; hours went by before the sun could disperse those vapours and warm and purify the villages.
>
> In New Mexico he always awoke a young man; not until he rose and began to shave did he realize that he was growing older. His first consciousness was a sense of the light dry wind blowing in through the windows, with the fragrance of hot sun and sage-brush and sweet clover; a wind that made one's body feel light and one's heart cry "To-day, to-day," like a child's.
>
> Beautiful surroundings, the society of learned men, the charm of noble women, the graces of art, could not make up to him for the loss of those light-hearted mornings of the desert, for that wind that made one a boy again. . . .

That air would disappear from the whole earth in time, perhaps; but long after his day. He did not know just when it had become so necessary to him, but he had come back to die in exile for the sake of it. Something soft and wild and free, something that whispered to the ear on the pillow, lightened the heart, softly, softly picked the lock, slid the bolts, and released the prisoned spirit of man into the wind, into the blue and gold, into the morning, into the morning![4]

That is just pure poetry, isn't it? Again, let the words have their way with you.

My second suggestion is that you learn to distinguish between true art and cheap substitutes. Let me say, now and forever, that rhyme does not a poem make. Rhyme may make a verse, but it does not make a poem. Rhyme is a part of many poems, but we do not make a poem by merely rhyming an idea. Literary art is the product of a gifted, creative, disciplined mind encountering experience and interpreting it through language. There is a perversity in many of us that makes us think that the best film or the best book is the one that makes us cry the most. For some reason we like the cathartic experience of tears, so we tend to think, "That was a marvelous book; I wept all the way through it." Some good books do have that effect on us, but that is not necessarily what makes them good. Some writers, some third-rate writers, know how to push certain buttons and get certain responses from us. They know we will weep if they talk about a poor, lost child or about a bad man who turns good and dies. But we should not go to books just for their tear-evoking power.

Mark Twain particularly despised sentimentalism in literature, and he had a great deal of fun attacking it in *Huckleberry Finn.* You might remember the occasion when Huck and Jim have been separated by an accident on the river, and Huck is rescued by the Grangerford family, who are true Southern nobility. They do everything proper—except that they have feuds and kill their neighbors, a minor consideration because they observe all the established conventions. Well, they had a daughter named Emmeline, now deceased, who was on hand at every death with a tear-jerking poem. It was said that when somebody died, the doctor arrived first, then Emmeline, and then the undertaker. But Huck explained that one time the undertaker arrived before Emmeline did—she was hung up on some difficult rhyme. After that she just pined away to an early death. Emmeline was also a painter, and here is Huck's description of some of Emmeline's paintings:

> They was different from any pictures I ever see before; blacker mostly, than is common. One was a woman in a slim black dress, belted small under the armpits, with bulges like a cabbage in the middle of the sleeves, and a large black scoop-shovel bonnet with black veil, and white slim ankles crossed about with black tape, and very wee black slippers, like a chisel, and she was leaning pensive on a tombstone on her right elbow, under a weeping willow, and her other hand hanging down her side holding a white handkerchief and a reticule, and underneath the picture it said "Shall I Never See Thee More, Alas."

Here is another one Huck describes:

> A young lady with her hair all combed up straight to the top of her head, and knotted there in front of a comb like a chair back, and she was crying into a handkerchief and had a dead bird laying on its back in her other hand with its heels up, and underneath the picture it said "I Shall Never Hear Thy Sweet Chirrup More Alas." There was one where a young lady was at a window looking up at the moon, and tears running down her cheeks; and she had an open letter in one hand with black sealing wax showing on one edge of it, and she was mashing a locket with a chain to it against her mouth, and underneath the picture it said "And Art Thou Gone Yes Thou Art Gone Alas." These was all nice pictures, I reckon, but I didn't somehow take to them, because if ever I was down a little, they always give me the fan-tods. Everybody was sorry she died, because she had laid out a lot more of these pictures to do, and a body could see by what she had done what they had lost. But I reckoned that with her disposition, she was having a better time in the graveyard.

186

Then Huck quotes one of Emmeline's deathbed poems. The title is "Ode to Stephen Dowling Bots, Deceased":

> And did young Stephen sicken,
> And did young Stephen die?
> And did the sad hearts thicken,
> And did the mourners cry?
>
> No; such was not the fate of
> Young Stephen Dowling Bots;
> Though sad hearts round him thicken,
> 'Twas not from sickness' shots.
>
> No whooping-cough did rack his frame,
> Nor measles drear, with spots;
> Not these impaired the sacred name
> Of Stephen Dowling Bots.
>
> Despised love struck not with woe
> That head of curly knots,
> Nor stomach troubles laid him low,
> Young Stephen Dowling Bots.
>
> Oh no. Then list with tearful eye,
> Whilst I his fate do tell,
> His soul did from this cold world fly,
> By falling down a well.
>
> They got him out and emptied him;
> Alas it was too late;
> His spirit was gone for to sport aloft
> In the realms of the good and great.[5]

A third-rate writer is likely to take a very legitimate subject and then cheapen it by taking the meaning out of it. There are a lot of sentimental poems in print. One that comes to mind is called "The Well-Aimed Tear." Picture, if you will, the writer of this poem writing and weeping, aiming his tear so that it will blend with somebody else's tear on a grave. He makes his calculations, takes aim, and drops the tear. There are too many poems of this sort; you know them too well. One problem with

the sentimental in literature is that instead of re-creating experience in which we can participate, it simply pushes the buttons
to call up experience we are already supposed to have had. An
honest piece of literature brings us to emotion by taking us
through experience.

By way of contrast with the sentimental pieces we just
noted, let me read a few passages from Shakespeare's *King
Lear*. In this play the emotion is earned. You may very well feel
like crying, but if you do, it is because you have lived with the
characters and seen them struggling. You remember that King
Lear is an imperious old king, proud, haughty, not always very
wise. He decides when he reaches his eighties that he is tired of
all the responsibilities of being king and that he should divide
his kingdom among his three daughters. He wants all the
privileges and trappings of kingship, but he does not want the
responsibilities anymore. He determines to make the division
according to the degree of love his daughters profess for him.
The two older daughters flatter him, telling him that they love
him immensely, but Cordelia, the younger daughter (who has a
streak of her father's stubbornness in her, I suspect) will not
play that game, although she genuinely loves him. She simply
says, "I love you as a daughter loves a father." He gets terribly
angry, divides the kingdom between the two wicked daughters,
and banishes Cordelia. As it turns out, the wicked daughters
strip him of his knights, his retinue, and the trappings of kingship, and finally drive him out onto the heath one terribly
stormy night. He is dispossessed of everything. He undergoes
great suffering, and even though he begins losing his mind, he
arrives at new wisdom.

As the play moves toward its close, a battle ensues between
Cordelia's forces (she has married the king of France) and the
forces of the wicked daughters. Cordelia and Lear come together again in a highly emotional moment. Lear, by this time, is
almost out of his mind; he is not even sure that he knows who
she is. Her first words to him when she sees him are: "How
does my royal Lord? How fares your Majesty?" (4.7.44). Here is
this man in shreds, half mad, stripped of everything, and what
does she call him? "My royal Lord" and "your Majesty." She still

speaks to him as if he were king. He responds, "Where have I been? Where am I? Fair daylight?" (4.7.52). As he tries to sort things out, he kneels before her. Imagine this old king on his knees, a man who would not have knelt to anybody at the beginning of the play. We realize how far he has come. She cannot bear to see him in such humiliation. She cries,

> O, look upon me, sir,
> And hold your hands in benediction o'er me.
> No, sir, you must not kneel. (Act IV, vii, 57-58)

To this King Lear responds,

> Pray, do not mock me:
> I am a very foolish fond old man. (IV, vii, 59-60)

What kind of an admission is that for him to make? He then continues:

> Fourscore and upward, not an hour more nor less;
> And, to deal plainly,
> I fear I am not in my perfect mind. (IV, vii, 61-63)

That kind of admission would have been impossible for him earlier. Then he says:

> Do not laugh at me;
> For, as I am a man, I think this lady
> To be my child Cordelia. (IV, vii, 68-70)

He has a sudden glimpse of recognition, and she replies, "And so I am, I am." (IV, vii, 70.) This is a marvelously moving scene. Then Lear says,

> Be your tears wet? yes, faith. I pray weep not:
> If you have poison for me, I will drink it.
> I know you do not love me; for your sisters
> Have, as I do remember, done me wrong:
> You have some cause, they have not. (IV, vii, 71-75)

And her broken reply is, "No cause, no cause." (IV, vii, 75.) How lovely is this coming together of father and daughter after so many years of wrongful separation.

The battle goes on, and the tides turn. Cordelia's forces are losing, and she and Lear are both taken prisoners. She is angry and impatient, eager to right the wrongs that have been done to Lear. But he is not interested in retribution right now. He has his beloved daughter back, and that is the most important thing to him now. He says,

> No, no, no, no! Come, let's away to prison:
> We two alone will sing like birds i' the cage:
> When thou dost ask me blessing, I'll kneel down
> And ask of thee forgiveness: so we'll live,
> And pray, and sing, and tell old tales, and laugh
> At gilded butterflies, and hear poor rogues
> Talk of court news; and we'll talk with them too
> Who loses and who wins, who's in, who's out;
> And take upon 's the mystery of things,
> As if we were God's spies: and we'll wear out,
> In a wall'd prison, packs and sects of great ones
> That ebb and flow by the moon. (V, iii, 8-19)

He says, essentially, that it is enough for him for them to be together, even if they are in prison. Lear has come a long way since the opening scenes.

Then the tide turns again. Cordelia's forces begin winning, but her execution has already been ordered. And before that order can be reversed, she is hanged. Lear enters, carrying her in his arms, crying,

> Howl, howl, howl, howl! O, you are men of stones:
> Had I your tongues and eyes, I'ld use them so
> That heaven's vault should crack. She's gone for ever!
> I know when one is dead and when one lives;
> She's dead as earth. Lend me a looking glass;
> If that her breath will mist or stain the stone,
> Why, then she lives. (V, iii, 257-63)

But he cannot quite accept her death. Even though he knows she is dead, he still must hope. As Lear is dying, he cries,

> And my poor fool is hang'd! No, no, no life!
> Why should a dog, a horse, a rat, have life,
> And thou no breath at all? Thou'lt come no more,
> Never, never, never, never, never! (V, iii, 306-9)

Then, just before he dies, hope glimmers again:

> Do you see this? Look on her! look! her lips!
> Look there, look there! (V, iii, 311-12)

At that moment he dies, thinking she may have been restored and indeed may be alive. Now that is earned emotion. What you feel as you read those lines is real.

My third suggestion is that when you are reading literature, you should seek its intellectual and spiritual illumination. That does not mean that we can look in literature for easy answers and soothing philosophies. The best literature does not contain very many easy answers, but it can lead us to a discovery of life's critical questions. The basic questions of human experience are questions like "Who am I?" "What is my relationship with God and the world?" and "What is my relationship with other human beings?"

In one of the classes I teach, we just read a book in which the character has made some very serious mistakes. He has chased after money and social position and a love that would bring these things with it. He wanders into a church and utters a very unusual prayer. One of the questions he asks in this prayer is, "What is it I have chosen?" All of us could ask that question about ourselves: "What is it I have chosen really? What is it I have worshipped?"

Let us turn for a moment to Emily Dickinson, who asks questions that appear to be very simple but that are, in fact, some of the hardest questions of all. Sometimes she asks them whimsically, as in this poem:

> I'm nobody! Who are you?
> Are you nobody, too?
> Then there's a pair of us—don't tell!
> They'd banish us, you know.

191

How dreary to be somebody!
How public, like a frog
To tell your name the livelong June
To an admiring bog![6]

She knew something about problems of identity. Playful as she is at times, at other times she is deadly serious. Note the difficult issues she raises in this deceptively simple poem:

I never lost as much but twice,
And that was in the sod;
Twice have I stood a beggar
Before the door of God!

Angels, twice descending,
Reimbursed my store.
Burglar, banker, father,
I am poor once more![7]

She says a great deal in just that one line: "Burglar, banker, father." Imagine the questions in Dickinson's mind. "Who is God? What is my relationship to him? Why does he take away? Why must my friends die?" In what sense is God both a burglar and a banker? He restores each time, and yet he takes away. And since he is also our Father, perhaps he loves us and cares about us. In those three words—"Burglar, banker, father"—Dickinson is pondering the roles of her Father in heaven and her relationship with him.

Emily Dickinson was terribly aware that in this life there are often no answers, or at least no simple answers, to many of our most difficult questions. Let me read another of her poems:

I heard a fly buzz when I died—
The stillness in the room
Was like the stillness in the air
Between the heaves of storm.
The eyes around had wrung them dry
And breaths were gathering firm
For that last onset when the King
Be witnessed in the room.

192

I will keep my keepsakes, signed away
What portion of me be
Assignable—
And then it was there interposed a fly,
With blue, uncertain, stumbling buzz,
Between the light and me.
And then the windows failed and then
I could not see to see.[8]

All of us expect that when the moment of transition to the hereafter comes, there will be light, illumination. We expect to understand the things we have not understood in this life. But Dickinson is suggesting that perhaps even then we will have no answers. Maybe there will interpose a fly between the light, or intelligence, and us. "And then the windows failed," the eyes closed, "and then I could not see to see." We may never know; how does one face that kind of possibility?

My fourth and final suggestion is that in literature we should seek for a revelation of human character. E. M. Forster, in a book called *Aspects of the Novel,* says that one reason we go to literature, one reason we enjoy it so much, is that we can know things about people in literature that we cannot know in real life. There are things about every one of us here that we have never told a soul. We all have our secret selves, selves perhaps even we do not understand, things that nobody knows but us. Forster says that the novelist tells us what a person is thinking, thereby revealing all of that person's characteristics. But, says Forster, "human intercourse, as soon as we look at it for its own sake and not as a social adjunct, is seen to be haunted by a spectre. We cannot understand each other, except in a rough and ready way; we cannot reveal ourselves, even when we want to; what we call intimacy is only a makeshift; perfect knowledge is an illusion. But in the novel we can know people perfectly." He says further that characters in novels "are people whose secret lives are visible or might be visible: we are people whose secret lives are invisible. And that is why novels, even when they are about wicked people, can solace us; they suggest a more comprehensible and thus a more manageable human race."[9] We like to find somebody we can understand.

Let us look at three characters from fiction to illustrate the great delight we can experience in learning to know another human being. This is one of Melville's descriptions of crazy Captain Ahab in *Moby Dick.* This is the man, you remember, who was compelled to pursue the great white whale:

> Socially, Ahab was inaccessible. Though nominally included in the census of Christendom, he was still an alien to it. He lived in the world, as the last of the Grisly Bears lived in settled Missouri. And as when the Spring and Summer had departed, that wild Logan of the woods, burying himself in the hollow of the tree, lived out the winter there, sucking his own paws, so, in his inclement, howling old age, Ahab's soul, shut up in the caved trunk of his body, there fed upon the sullen paws of its gloom![10]

Isn't that a magnificent figure of speech, comparing Ahab to an old bear who sits walled in, sustaining himself by sucking on his own paws? It is a remarkable characterization. Not all literature is as serious as *Moby Dick,* however. Those who have read Eudora Welty know how much fun she can be. In a little novel called *The Ponder Heart,* a character called Edna Earl Ponder tells the story. She runs the local hotel, and she is talking someone's ear off through the whole novel. This is what she says:

> I was up there in my room, reading some directions. That's something I find I like to do when I have a few minutes to myself—I don't know about you. How to put on furniture polish, transfer patterns with a hot iron, take off corns, I don't care what it is. I don't have to *do* it. Sometimes I'd rather sit still a minute and read a good quiet set of directions through than any story you'd try to wish off on me.[11]

I don't know about you, but I read cereal boxes in the morning.

Here is another marvelous example, this one from Flannery O'Connor's story "Good Country People." She is introducing Mrs. Freeman, one of the characters in the story:

> Besides the neutral expression that she wore when she was alone, Mrs. Freeman had two others, forward and

reverse, that she used for all her human dealings. Her forward expression was steady and driving like the advance of a heavy truck. Her eyes never swerved to left or right but turned as the story turned as if they followed a yellow line down the center of it. She seldom used the other expression because it was not often necessary for her to retract a statement, but when she did, her face came to a complete stop, there was an almost imperceptible movement of her black eyes, during which they seemed to be receding, and then the observer would see that Mrs. Freeman, though she might stand there as real as several grain sacks thrown on top of each other, was no longer there in spirit.

The woman Mrs. Freeman is talking with in the kitchen that day is almost her match. Her name is Mrs. Hopewell: "Mrs. Hopewell had no bad qualities of her own but she was able to use other people's in such a constructive way that she never felt the lack." This is how Mrs. Hopewell talks: "Nothing is perfect. This was one of Mrs. Hopewell's favorite sayings. Another was: That's life! And still another, the most important, was: Well, other people have their opinions too."[12]

You would love Mrs. Hopewell's daughter. Mrs. Hopewell named her Joy, but she renamed herself Hulga. Hulga has a wooden leg, and in this story she decides that she is going to seduce a young Bible salesman who is nineteen years old. She has a Ph.D. in philosophy, she is in her early thirties, and she is a mean one. They arrange to go on a picnic together, she in her yellow sweatshirt, he with his satchel of Bibles. She manages to climb a ladder to the loft of a barn, and the two of them begin talking and hugging. She assumes he is terribly innocent, but when he opens the case that supposedly contains Bibles, we discover that it is full of whiskey and obscene playing cards. As it turns out, he is the one who intends to do the seducing. He sweet-talks her into letting him remove her wooden leg, and then he runs off with it. Hulga looks at him in stunned disbelief and says, "Aren't you just good country people?" He knows more about wickedness than she ever did.

The interesting thing about this story is that O'Connor said she just started writing this story about two women she knew,

Mrs. Freeman with the neutral, forward, and reverse expressions, and Mrs. Hopewell. She claims that she did not even know that the Bible salesman was going to steal the wooden leg until ten lines before he did it. Then she said she realized that it was inevitable. Most certainly, writers work by inspiration and even whim.

In conclusion, let me stress that in art and literature lies the affirmation of ourselves as human beings. I really believe that the most important legacy that one generation leaves to succeeding generations is the legacy of art. It is our best artifact, isn't it? The finest that has been thought and felt throughout time—that is what literature is, as Matthew Arnold defined it. How much poorer we would be if Milton and Shakespeare and a host of others had never lived and never written. Too often we think of poverty only in economic terms. I suggest that there is such a thing as poverty of the spirit, and that kind of poverty strikes the rich as well as the poor.

Let me conclude with one last Dickinson poem:

> He ate and drank the precious Words—
> His Spirit grew robust—
> He knew no more that he was poor,
> Nor that his frame was Dust—
>
> He danced along the dingy Days
> And this Bequest of Wings
> Was but a Book—What liberty
> A loosened spirit brings—[13]

I pray that we may all find in books the liberty that a "loosened spirit" brings.

Notes

1. Edwin Arlington Robinson, "Miniver Cheevy," in *Selected Poems of Edwin Arlington Robinson* (New York: The Macmillan Co., 1931), pp. 87-88.
2. Henry David Thoreau, *Walden* (Columbus, Ohio: Charles E. Merrill Publishing Co., 1969), pp. 5-6.
3. *Antony and Cleopatra,* Act II, scene 2, lines 196-223.
4. Willa Cather, *Death Comes for the Archbishop* (New York: Alfred A. Knopf, 1927), pp. 276-77.

5. Mark Twain, *The Adventures of Huckleberry Finn* (New York: Grossett Dunlap, 1948), pp. 86-89.
6. Emily Dickinson, *The Complete Works of Emily Dickinson,* Thomas H. Johnson, ed. (London: Faber and Faber Limited, 1960), p. 658.
7. Dickinson, pp. 1012-13.
8. Dickinson, p. 1019.
9. E. M. Forster, *Aspects of the Novel* (New York: Harcourt Brace Jovanovich, 1965), pp. 62-65.
10. Herman Melville, *Moby Dick* (New York: Franklin Watts), pp. 214, 215.
11. Eudora Welty, *The Ponder Heart* (New York: Harcourt Brace Jovanovich, 1954), pp. 52-53.
12. Flannery O'Connor, *The Complete Stories* (New York: Farrar, Straus, Giroux, 1971), pp. 271-74.
13. Emily Dickinson, *The Poems of Emily Dickinson* (Cambridge, Massachusetts: Belknap Press, 1955), p. 64.

Marilyn Arnold was graduated with highest honors from Brigham Young University and received a Ph.D. in American literature from the University of Wisconsin. She is dean of the Graduate School at BYU.

Appendix
The American Woman's Movement

BELLE S. SPAFFORD

*T*he intensity of activity in recent years on the part of certain women's groups, as well as on the part of some individual women, in behalf of improving the status of women and removing what they regard as injustices, has been called by one editorial writer "the sensation of the hour." The goals women's groups seek and the general interest of the public in what is happening are reflected in numerous newspaper and magazine articles, in bulletins, in radio and television programs, in editorials, in conference and seminar programs, and in other ways. For example, I assembled at random seventeen headlines from newspapers, magazines, and bulletins that were close at hand as I began preparation for this talk. To illustrate the nature of the articles, I cite a few headlines:

1. "Report Shows Women Still Suffer Discrimination at National and International Levels in Education, Government, and Private Industry"

This address was given in July 1974 at the Lochinvar Club in New York City.

2. "Women Charge Discrimination in University Admission Policies and Scholarship Grants"
3. "Women Seek Ordination to the Ministry"
4. "Women Students Urged to Reach for Training in Traditionally Male Dominated Fields"
5. "Give Women Credit Where Credit Is Due" (referring to purchasing credit)
6. "Women Emerging as New Breed of Political Activists"

One brave man published an article entitled "Women Filling Men's Jobs." The writer inquired, "What will this do to me and my ilk?"

Three major questions arise. First, are we in the midst of a new movement? Second, what has given rise to today's agitation? Third, what does it portend?

It is my opinion, based on some research and many years of identification with organized women, both nationally and internationally, that the current effort commonly referred to as "Women's Lib" is an offshoot of what began in the early part of the nineteenth century. Traditionally, the activity has been referred to as "The Woman's Movement."

As times have changed and progress has been made in the lot of women, new demands have come to the fore, and agitation that they be met has been intensified in recent years.

To review the rise of the American woman since the 1830s, which is generally conceded to have had its faint beginnings at that time, is to see her taking part in one of the great dramas of the ages. It is to see a tremendous force, which had been partially dormant, brought into active exercise in the great work of the world. She moved onto the stage of this great drama when there was need for her intuition and intelligent service.

In colonial days women had more rights socially and politically than in the days of the early republic. In the matter of the franchise, colonial women usually had the right to vote. It is doubtful, however, whether they made much use of the privilege. A few women, as individuals, did distinguish themselves in fields outside the home. The American Revolution produced women like Abigail Adams, whose letters and pamphlets, history tells us, "helped light the fires that blazed at Concord."

Following the Revolution, there was a dull interregnum in the life of the American woman. For almost half a century she seemed to have stood still. One historical writer declared that women were as silent as the tomb. They probably were held less important in the social scheme than they had ever been before or were destined ever to be again.

In 1833 there began faint stirrings. A silent revolution was beginning to take form insofar as woman and her privileges and her work were concerned. In the early part of the nineteenth century, Eli Whitney invented the cotton gin. It revived the slumping institution of slavery, which was growing increasingly distasteful to many women, who by nature were endowed with humanitarian impulses. Weaving came out of the home, taking with it numbers of women to work at the industrial power looms. The industrial revolution was being born. This and the distaste for slavery are generally regarded as being behind the stirrings of the women for greater freedom of action and better opportunities for education. Education for women at that time was confined, in the main, to the three Rs.

In 1833 an American institution of higher learning, Oberlin College of Ohio, under pressure we are told, opened its doors to women. It established a kind of annex, a female department, entitled "Collegiate Institute." The announcement had its pathos, its humor, and its general touch of patronage. The reason given for the action was: "The elevation of the female character by bringing within the reach of the misguided and neglected sex the instruction privileges which had hitherto distinguished the leading sex from theirs." (Inez Haynes Irwin, *Angels and Amazons* [Doubleday and Doran Company, 1933], p. 39.) Fifteen women enrolled.

In 1833 there appeared the first women's club to which one might apply the term in its modern meaning, "The Ladies Association for the Education of Females" of Jacksonville, Illinois. Then came "The Female Anti-Slavery Society." Both organizations were short lived.

An interesting story is recorded in a book titled *Angels and*

Amazons, by Inez H. Irwin, in reference to a world antislavery conference held in London in 1840. The United States sent delegates, among them William Lloyd Garrison, who was expected to make the great speech of the occasion. Henry B. Stanton took with him his bride, Elizabeth Cady Stanton, and a few other women who were deputized as delegates, among them Lucretia Mott and Elizabeth Peace. When the American women tried to take their seats, the conference denied them recognition. After a long and agitated discussion, the house compromised by deciding that the women might not take part in the proceedings, but might sit behind a screen in the gallery and listen. William Lloyd Garrison, arriving late, acted with characteristic justice and generosity. He promptly took his seat with his country's women and insisted on listening with them. He did not make his speech.

The event that perpetuates this conference in history, however, happened outside the hall and had nothing to do with black slavery. Hurt and righteously indignant, Lucretia Mott and Elizabeth Cady Stanton walked down Great Queen Street that night, discussing the burning injustice of the day's proceedings. At home these two women had struggled against the handicap of having to keep silent. Now in England, which had already manumitted her black slaves, behind a screen they faced facts at last. They drew a logical conclusion that they should go back to America and begin agitation for women's rights. This was a highlight in the history of feminism. (Irwin, pp. 78-79.)

With the dawn of the 1840s there appears to have been a general awakening with regard to the power of organization and the need for it.

In 1842 a unique and significant event took place. A handful of women, members of a newly organized church, The Church of Jesus Christ of Latter-day Saints, residing in Nauvoo, Illinois (a western frontier town), approached the Prophet Joseph Smith, who presided over the Church. They appealed to him to organize them in order that they might more effectively serve the Church and the people generally. The response of the Prophet to the request was favorable. On March 17 of that year, the Female Relief Society of Nauvoo, now known as the Relief

Society of The Church of Jesus Christ of Latter-day Saints, was organized according to parliamentary procedures. The major purposes of the organization were defined as education (with emphasis on religious education), the development of women, and benevolent service. (On the flyleaf of the first volume of a biography titled *Life and Works of Susan B. Anthony,* presented to the Relief Society, the author, Ida H. Harper, wrote this statement, "All honor to the Relief Society of The Church of Jesus Christ of Latter-day Saints, the first organized charity." It may be of interest to you that on the flyleaf of volume 2 of the same work, presented to the Relief Society, the author in her own handwriting states, "To the women who were loyal and helpful to Miss Anthony to the end of her great work.")

Orderly procedures were marked out for maintaining and conducting the affairs of the Society. Under the direction of the presiding priesthood of the Church, the women were "authorized to direct, control, and govern the affairs of the society . . . in the sphere assigned to it." (Bruce R. McConkie, *Relief Society Magazine,* March 1950, p. 150.)

Latter-day Saint women from the very beginning of the Church had held a position of dignity, trust, and responsibility. Their mental capacities were recognized, as was their right to develop their talents to the full. They had been given the religious vote almost with the founding of the Church in 1830. Elsewhere, this was at a time when few men and no women enjoyed this privilege. Now, these women had been given the unique recognition of having an organization of their own, a structure through which to advance themselves and give service.

At the third meeting of the Society, the Prophet Joseph Smith met with the women. In addressing them, he made this significant statement: "I now turn the key in your behalf in the name of the Lord, and this Society shall rejoice, and knowledge and intelligence shall flow down from this time henceforth; this is the beginning of better days to the poor and needy, who shall be made to rejoice and pour forth blessings on your heads."

I have already referred to the limited educational opportunities for women extant at that time. Insofar as the needy were concerned, there were few private agencies for the care of the dependent, and public provisions afforded but one type of treatment—custody only for the poor, the feebleminded, the insane, and the miscreant. Almshouse care was considered to be the most satisfactory method of providing for the poor.

As we consider our great systems of education today, as well as our vast private and public welfare systems, we must concede that this small group of organized women had listened that day to inspired words.

With reference to the words "turn the key" in behalf of women, to turn a key implies to open a door. Opening a door contemplates a structure built for some specific purpose, with doors through which people pass in using the structure for the purposes for which it was designed. It is my conviction that the words "turn the key" for women implied opening doors of opportunity and advancement for them through the structure of an organization. It is my further conviction, shared by others, that the key was turned not alone for Relief Society women, but for women worldwide.

For those of us who believe in the overruling power of a Supreme Being in the affairs of mankind, it does not seem inconsistent to accept the words "I now turn the key" as divine afflatus in relation to women; nor in the light of future events does it seem unreasonable to regard this action as the actual beginning of organized effort for woman's emancipation from restraints that for years had encumbered her full development and usefulness.

Today [1974] the Relief Society, founded in 1842 with a membership of eighteen women, is national and international in scope. It operates in seventy countries of the world and has on its rolls the names of approximately 1.5 million women eighteen years of age and over, representing many nationalities. Its membership includes non-Latter-day Saint women as well as Latter-day Saint women, for the Society maintains an open-door membership policy. Its programs and instructional materials are now translated into sixteen different languages. Insofar as we are able to determine, the Relief Society is the oldest national women's organization to continuously persist.

And now as to what followed: In 1848, six years after the

founding of the Relief Society, what is regarded as the first women's rights convention was held in the little Wesleyan church in Seneca Falls, New York. It was practically a small assembly of neighbors, but it threshed out the first Declaration of Independence for Women, demanding for them educational, industrial, social, and political rights.

During the next forty years, organizations flourished in numbers. In 1888 the National Woman's Suffrage Association convened, in Washington, D.C., what is regarded by many women's organizations as the greatest women's convention ever held. It was called, so they announced, to observe the fortieth anniversary of the first public declaration of women's rights. The underlying purpose, however, was to further the cause of woman's suffrage.

Invitations to this convention were issued to seventy-seven women's organizations, selected as being either national in scope or of national value. Of this number, fifty-three accepted, among them the Relief Society. (It may be of interest to you to know that Utah women had been granted suffrage in 1870 and were conspicuous figures in the national woman's suffrage movement.) In addition to the delegates from the United States, there were in attendance representatives from England, France, Norway, Denmark, India, Finland, and Canada. Eighty speakers addressed the convention, but the central figure proved to be Susan B. Anthony. One of her biographers said of her, "In her black dress and pretty red silk shawl, with her gray-brown hair smoothly combed over a regal head, [she was] worthy of any statesman." (Ida Husted Harper, *Life and Works of Susan B. Anthony,* 1898, 2:638.)

In addressing the meeting preliminary to the convention, Susan B. Anthony, with all the earnestness of her strong nature and with her voice vibrating with emotion, set farsighted views with regard to the platform. Said Mrs. Anthony: "We have now come to another turning-point and, if it is necessary, I will fight forty years more to make our platform free for the Christian to stand upon whether she be a Catholic and counts her beads, or a Protestant of the straitest orthodox creed. . . . These are the principles I want you to maintain, that our platform may be kept as broad as the universe, that upon it may stand the representatives of all creeds and no creeds—Jew or Christian, Protestant or Catholic, Gentile or Mormon, pagan or atheist." (Harper, 2:631.)

The chief outcome of this convention was the formation of the National Council of Women of the United States, to be made up of national women's organizations or of organizations whose programs were of national import, and the formation of the International Council of Women, to be made up of national councils of the respective nations. Both organizations are active and influential today.

Dedicating themselves to the cause of suffrage, these organized women swung into vigorous action. It was not until 1920, however, that the Nineteenth Amendment to the United States Constitution was adopted, granting to women of the U.S. the right to vote and to hold public office.

Women, however, appear to have been somewhat slow to expand their role in society, even after having been granted the franchise and other opportunities they had demanded in their own declaration of independence. This was due, I believe, to a recognition of their lack of adequate training and experience in public life.

We recall also that war had descended upon the world, World War I followed by World War II. The wars seemed to entice, if not force, women out of their homes and into the labor market. After World War II an interesting phenomenon occurred in the world of work. A good portion of the women who, as a patriotic duty during the war years, had taken jobs, many of which were traditionally uncommon to women, felt a new independence; they saw advantages in the paycheck, and many of them never went back to the home and the life of a full-time housewife.

The desire of women to remain in the labor market and upgrade their employment opportunities was soon accompanied by an intense desire for training and education to qualify them for better job opportunities and a wider variety of services. The effort to thus upgrade employment opportunities continues.

According to a study made by a staff of researchers at the Columbia Broadcasting System, more than fifteen million women in the United States today have at least some college training, more than twice as many as two decades ago. Concomitant with this training, there exist more and better work opportunities. In addition, the prevailing attitude toward smaller families, the rapid technological improvements affecting housework, together with economic need influenced by inflation, have pushed increasing numbers of married women into the work force.

With this there have developed new demands by women for greater recognition, a determination to stamp out job discrimination on the basis of their sex, and agitation for increased opportunities in the top policy and decision-making levels of public life. As I assess it, recently we have been passing through a period of upheaval. Agitation began with a few sporadic efforts by poorly structured groups, somewhat militant in character and extreme in viewpoints, gaining momentum until it has now become a national effort, commonly referred to as the Women's Liberation Movement. Presently there are a number of well-structured organizations with dedicated members and determined goals. Militancy has largely subsided, although, in my opinion, some extremism remains.

Among the big issues that appear to stand out are the demand for full equality with men in opportunities and rights, the determination to wipe out the traditional obeisance to the concept of male supremacy, and the intent to completely eradicate everything that tends toward denying woman full identity as a person or toward placing her in a position where she may be regarded as a second-class citizen.

The efforts to achieve these goals are being accompanied, in some instances, by shifts in some of the traditional values of life. Certain sacred patterns of life that have proved rewarding to both men and women and socially stabilizing, such as marriage laws and covenants, are feeling the impact. Certain new philosophies with regard to the character of home and family life are being aired that run counter to the time-tested traditional values. While the number of liberal advocates appears to be limited, their views are proving controversial. I cite a few of these views as examples:

1. The advocacy of de facto marriage (i.e., actually existing without legal action).

2. The attempt to eliminate male domination in monogamous marriage. There are those who affirm that legally monogamous marriage is the most male-dominated institution of all, and is the only institution in which women are expected to work without receiving any stipulated wage, as well as without having fixed working hours.

3. The determination to "throttle" the overproduction of babies. One viewpoint declares, "It's not women's lib that is downgrading the motherhood role; it is the ever more visible fact of overpopulation, and a reduction in the occupation of motherhood is now mandatory."

4. The efforts to curb the existing excessive voluntary service by women. The position of the advocates of this is that the volunteer worker robs another woman, who needs paid employment, of a job opportunity.

Some pollsters find that women in large numbers prefer the job of wife and homemaker to that of the unmarried woman working and seeking fulfillment in man's competitive working world. They prefer the gratification of motherhood, the privileges of wifehood, the position generally accorded the woman in the home by family members, and the status conferred by society on the title *Mrs.* Some activists have openly stated that one of their big problems is the indifference of the average married woman to their efforts to liberate her from her traditional status of housewife.

The home and family are not alone in feeling the impact of new views and current demands. They are also being felt by business, education, and other institutions, along with government, as these institutions endeavor wisely to adapt to new concepts and new demands.

Withal, there are some things for which women are agitating that merit support: for example, equal pay for equal work and nondiscrimination in hiring practices when a male and a female applicant are equally qualified.

Personally, I am not in accord with those who believe that current problems and needs of women may best be answered by adoption of a constitutional amendment on equal rights. I am of the opinion that major advantages embodied in the proposed amendment could be achieved through regular channels of state and federal legislative action without raising questionable results. I believe further that by nature, men and women differ physically, biologically, and emotionally, and that the greatest good to the individual and society results where these differences are respected in the divisions of labor in the home as well as in community life.

Working with women in many countries of the world convinces me that there is no task to which woman may put her hand so broad and inspiring, so filled with interest, so demanding of intelligence and capability, so rewarding, as that of wife, mother, and homemaker. I regard this role as taking precedence over all others for women. In a well-ordered home, husband and wife approach their responsibilities as a joint endeavor. Together they safeguard the sanctity of the home. Their personal relationship is characterized by respect and enduring love. They cherish their children. In child rearing, I believe, there is no substitute for a caring mother.

A woman should feel free, however, to go into the marketplace and into community services on a paid or volunteer basis if she so desires, when her home and family circumstances allow her to do so without impairment to her family life. Women owe it to themselves to develop their full potential as women—to exercise their mental capacities, to enlarge upon their talents, and to increase their skills—in order that they may give to the world the best they have in a manner that will produce the most good, regardless of the paths their lives may take.

I deplore the far-out views that openly break with those practices and procedures whose tested values over generations of time have contributed to the decency, stability, well-being, and happiness of humankind. I accept the premise that moral right is that which is true, ethically good and proper, and in conformity with moral law. What was morally right based on truth must remain right regardless of changing times and circumstances. Truth—and right that is based on truth—is immutable. We cannot afford to allow national sensitivity to become dulled into a calm acceptance of degenerating values and their demoralizing effects on our nation and its people.

What of tomorrow? I ask.

May I submit a few opinions, not that I regard myself in the slightest degree as a seer, but merely from the point of view of trends as I observe them and as I draw upon the past as I have noted it.

Just as the pendulum swings to and fro under the combined action of gravity and momentum to regulate the movements of clockworks and machinery, and usually with the first push strikes hard at the far left and far right, moving somewhat irregularly, and then finds its level, thus assuring the proper functioning of the instrument—so I believe will the pendulum of the current woman's action program perform.

Furthermore, I believe that without doubt many of the repressions and injustices that are troubling women today will be resolved. Gratefully, this is already taking place. I cite such things as equal pay for equal work under similar circumstances, new legislation on such things as property rights, and nondiscriminating credit laws. This portends a better day ahead for women.

Borrowing words from Marvin Kalb, "We have no valid evidence that today's headlines will be tomorrow's wisdom." Undoubtedly some of the things for which women are clamoring today will be in the discard tomorrow.

Tomorrow we undoubtedly will hear less of woman's rights and more of her responsibilities and achievements. Legislation may make legal the total equality of the sexes, but it is my opinion that the different natures of man and woman will be the supreme law in dictating the divisions of labor to which each will be drawn in the work of the world.

It is my experience that life, the stern teacher and the great disciplinarian, is now forcing upon us a recognition of the importance of spiritual and moral values. I believe a new day will find us moving forward toward primal religious, spiritual, and moral values, with materialism taking a lesser position. Man cannot live by bread alone.

I am convinced that the home will stand, as it has stood during past generations, as the cornerstone of a good society and a happy citizenry. While old activity patterns within the home may be modified by the impact of change outside the home, the enduring values that cannot be measured in terms of their monetary worth, their power for good, the need of the human being for them (such values as peace, security, love, understanding) will not be sacrificed on the altar of new philosophies and new concepts. Countless men and women and even children who have tasted these fruits of home and family life will recognize new philosophies that create spoilage in them, and they will fend them off. It is in the home that the lasting values of life are best internalized in the individual. It is this that builds good citizens, and good citizens make good nations.

President Spencer W. Kimball of The Church of Jesus Christ of Latter-day Saints has expressed the belief that the future of the nation, its success, and its development are based largely upon the strength of family life. I am confident there are tens of thousands of Americans, men and women, who share this belief.

Robert O'Brien, senior editor of *Reader's Digest,* had this to say in an address given in May 1974 at a conference of the American Mothers Committee, Inc., in New York City: "In our hearts, we all know that the home is the cornerstone of American democracy. . . . It's well that the nation recognize and remember it, and engrave it upon the tablets of her history." Throughout the ages children have needed mothers with their love and understanding guidance, men have needed wives, and women have needed husbands to share in the concerns and responsibilities of life. They have needed the happy, loving, and protective companionship of one another. It will ever be so.

There is an old saying, "Man must work while woman must wait." The waiting period for the wheels of progress to roll around in behalf of woman (a period during which woman herself has worked as well as waited) is now nearly over. We may now say to her, in the words of Solomon, the wise man of Israel, "Give her of the fruit of her hands; and let her own works praise her in the gates." (Proverbs 31:31.)

Belle S. Spafford served as general president of the Relief Society for twenty-nine years and president of the National Council of Women for a three-year term. She received an honorary doctorate as well as the Exemplary Womanhood Award from Brigham Young University.

Index

Adam, 59, 86
Advertising, 105-6
Affleck, Afton, 85-86
Affliction, 120
Aggressive behavior, 126, 128
Aging, 108, 115
Agitation and depression, 158-59
Agony and the Ecstasy, 51-52
Alcoholism, 111, 159
Alienation. *See* Loneliness
Anger, 131, 169-72
Anthony, Susan B., 205-6
Antidepressants, 161-62
Antony and Cleopatra, 183
Appearances, outward, 39-40, 107
Assertiveness, 125-33
Association of Mormon Counselors
    and Psychotherapists, 169, 172, 175
Atonement, 11, 36, 59-60
Attitudes, 29, 127-28, 132
Authority in the Church, 50

Baby given to wrong mother, 71
Baby food, father who ate, 60-61
Balance and mental health, 150-51;
    and depression, 172, 175
Baptism, meaning of, 66-69
Barrenness, 116
Bellows, Maggie, 14
Blessings for obedience, 63
Blueprints, example of, 27-28, 32, 35,
    37, 41
Books, 5-6, 9, 104, 181-97
Bread, homemade, banned by
    husband, 22

Brigham Young University, 1-2, 108-9,
    118
Building, process of, 28, 32

Careers, 95-96
Charity, 35, 41. *See also* Service
Childhood, importance of, 30
Childlike, becoming, 178
Children: spending time with, 30;
    teaching roles to, 48; Irish, 91;
    nurturing of, 98; independence of,
    115; of God, all are, 116; praying
    for, 122
Choices: conflicting, 22; influence of
    values on, 29; of adults, 30-31;
    family related, 40; personal, 41;
    making informed, 48; making
    right, 52-53, 55; exercising free, 85;
    weighing of, 96
Christ: becoming like, 46-47, 102,
    106-7; name of, 69-70; living as, 74,
    84; elder brother is, 86; birth of,
    101; teachings of, 102, 107, 110,
    112; center life on, 113, 174-75;
    light of, 137; anger of, 170-71
Church presidents: wives of, 109;
    mothers of, 119-20
Communication and assertiveness,
    126
Community, involvement in, 85-99
Compliments, article on, 17
Concentration, lack of, and depression,
    157-58
Counseling, to overcome depression,
    163, 173, 174

Death Comes for the Archbishop,
  183-84
Decision making, 20, 22, 28-29, 40
Degn, Louise, 151-52
Depression: treatment of, 153;
  commonness of, 154; women
  prone to, 154-55; symptoms of,
  155-59; recognition of, 159; causes
  of, 160; stress related, 161;
  reactive, 162-63
"Depression and Mormon Women,"
  151-52
Dickinson, Emily, 191-93, 196
Discipleship, 142
Discrimination of women, 207
Drifting in Church activity, 53-54
Drug abuse and depression, 159
Drunk drivers, 92

Education for women, 9, 30, 73, 201,
  203-4
Equal Rights Amendment, 209
Equality of sexes, 44-45
Eve, 82, 86

Faith, 54-55
Family: importance of, 3-7; comparing
  with others, 23
Fashion vs. fad, 37-38, 40
Father and son, communication
  between, 126-27
Feminism, 96, 202
Foundations, building, 32
Free agency, 140, 167, 175-76

Grandma, story of death of, 85
Grant, Heber J., 119
Guidelines to achieve goals, 176
Guilt: dealing with, 22-23; alleviation
  of, 25; burdens of, 97; overcoming,
  98; real and imagined, 118;
  depression and, 155

Handicapped woman, 88-89
Health: physical, importance of, 37;
  mental, 149-80
Holy Ghost, gifts of, 70-71
Huckleberry Finn, 185-87

Individual, worth of. *See* Self-esteem
Ireland, experience of women in,
  90-91

Jesus Christ. *See* Christ
Job, 168-69
Journalist who dies of lung cancer,
  14

Kimball, Spencer W., 119; struggle of,
  for self-worth, 16-17, 18; boy
  named after, 70; trials of, 167-68
Kimball, Spencer W., quotations from:
  on wife's education, 19; on role of
  women, 47-48, 61, 84, 97; on
  righteous women, 49-50; on
  achievement, 55; story of Bolivian
  woman, 60; on faithful women, 63,
  76; on service, 87; "Do it," 93; on
  his mother, 118-19; on wife's
  scripture study, 122; on spiritual
  development, 149; on family life,
  211
King Benjamin, 58-59, 69
King Lear, 188-91
Knowledge: pursuit of, 8, 112, 140

Labor, meanings of, 121
Lake, Louise, 88-89
Lawn mowing, example of, 126
Lee, Freda Joan, 109
Lee, Harold B.: quotations by, 16-17,
  50, 111, 122; mother of, 119
Lightner, Candy, 92
Literature, 9, 181-97
Love: God's, 11; self, 16-18, 173;
  brotherly, 18, 40, 132; mother's,
  116; unconditional, 174

Magdalene, Mary, 78
Marriage, temple, 3, 31, 44
McKay, David O.: quotations from, 3,
  116, 122; mother of, 119
Media, images of women in, 105-7
Medications, treatment of depression
  with, 161-62
Michelangelo, 51-52, 65-66
Missionary, influence of mother on,
  72
Moby Dick, 194
Mother Teresa, 82
Mothers: importance of, 5, 211;
  working, 6; divine mission of, 57;
  and fathers, 76; competent, 111; of
  Church presidents, 119; role of,
  122; modern views on, 208

Mott, Lucretia, 202
Movies, negative influences in, 106-7

Naomi, 78
National Council of Women, 93-94, 206
National Woman's Suffrage Association, 205

O'Connor, Flannery, 194-96
Obedience, importance of, 58-59, 63; blind, 150, 157-60

Partnership between men and women, 45, 76, 84
Patti Perfect, 149-50, 164-65, 169-70, 176
Physical cause of depression, 158-59
Polygamy, sisterhood in, 81-82
Prayer, 121-22
Priesthood; blessings of, for women, 56-57; and sisterhood, 75-84
Progression, eternal, 24, 36, 112

Refrigerator car, man locked in, 19
Relationships with others, 29
Relief Society, 80, 87, 93, 110, 202-4
Role models, 46, 78, 82
Ruth, example of, 78

Sarah, example of, 116-17
Scripture study, 135-47
Self-esteem, 16-18, 20, 108-10, 165-66, 173-74, 176-77
Service: to fellowmen, 3, 62-63, 85-99; be faithful in, 8; personal development through, 35; outside the home, 110-12; callings to, in Church, 177
Shakespeare, William, 183, 188, 196
Sisterhood, relationship of, to priesthood, 75-84
Smith, Emma, 80

Smith, George Albert, 93-94
Smith, Joseph: quotations by, 8, 48; first vision of, 43; women organized by, 45, 110, 202-3; anger of, 170
Smith, Joseph F., 120
Smith, Joseph Fielding, 119
Smith, Mary Fielding, 120
Snow, Eliza R., 33, 63, 110
Spafford, Belle S.: story about, 93-94; explains women's movement, 199-212
Spirit, influence of, 60
Stanton, Elizabeth Cady, 202
Stereotyping of boys and girls, 97-98, 104-5, 127
Suicide and depression, 156-57
Superwoman, article on, 95

TV, stereotypes on, 105-7
Tabitha, 145-46
Teresa, Mother, 82
Textbooks, stereotyping in, 104-5
Today, living for, 13-15
Travel, benefits of, 9-10
Twelve tribes, 144-45

Visiting teaching, 7-8
Volunteerism, 87
Vote, women gain right to, 206

Washington temple, experience in, 67-68
Wells, Emmeline B., 110
Welty, Eudora, 194
White child in black school, 117
Women's movement, 45, 95, 199-212
Woolf, Virginia, 83
Wordsworth, William, 16
Workaholics and depression, 159
Working women, 6-7, 31, 206, 209

Young, Brigham, 120, 150